The Blissful Union

Marriages are made in heaven, but the journey is covered on Earth. Enhance your chances to unite with your spouse in Jannah.

by

Syed Nooruzzuha Barmawar
Umm Amra Noora Jukaku

Introduction by:
Grand Mufti. Islamic Affairs. Dubai
Shaykh Dr. Mohammed Eyada Al-kobaisi

The Blissful Union ©2017 Syed ISBN 978-93-5268-923-1

The Blissful Union ©2017 Syed ISBN 978-93-5268-923-1

First Edition

ISBN 978-93-5268-923-1

INDEX

The Blissful Union ©2017 Syed ISBN 978-93-5268-923-1

The Blissful Union ©2017 Syed ISBN 978-93-5268-923-1

The Blissful Union ©2017 Syed ISBN 978-93-5268-923-1

The Blissful Union ©2017 Syed ISBN 978-93-5268-923-1

The Blissful Union ©2017 Syed ISBN 978-93-5268-923-1

Foreword

In the name of Allah, the Most Beneficent, the Most Merciful.

Due to the growing need of acquiring authentic Islamic knowledge regarding marriage, conjugal relations and dealing with one's spouse, we decided to write this book with hopes to benefit the Muslim *Ummah*, especially the youth.

Considering the state of the *Ummah* with increasing cases of divorce and the rise in *Haram* relationships and infidelity, this book will help muslims throughout the world to solve many issues and problems related to their marital life *In-sha-Allah*.

There are many etiquettes regarding love, marriage and intimacy that one needs to know and many aspects of those etiquettes have been covered in this book in the light of the Quran and *Hadith*. It will immensely benefit those who have questions with regards to conjugal and sexual relations between husband and wife and are otherwise shy to ask someone who possesses knowledge. Islam is a realistic religion and there is no shyness in *Deen* about matters that are necessary to live one's life.

The book is divided into topics dealing with various issues of love, marriage and intimacy. References for all the quotes have been provided mentioning volume, page and *hadith* number. We have strictly adhered to authentic *ahadith* which are either *Saheeh* or *Hasan*. Also, the stories of pious predecessors mentioned in this book are established with authentic chains. The scientific researches are quoted from renowned established journals citing volume and page number. The book ends with a conclusion, glossary of Islamic terminology and detailed bibliography.

The Blissful Union ©2017 Syed ISBN 978-93-5268-923-1

We thank Allah, the Most High, for giving us the ability and strength to prepare this work. We have tried our best to explain the matters related to marital and sexual relationships with clarity. We would like to thank Wahiba Naeem, Abdul Bari Khan and Mohammed Ammar for their suggestions and careful editing of the text. We are grateful to Suhail bin Sayeed for making software application of this book and Abdullah Taha for his valuable remarks. We ask Allah to make this work purely for His sake and accept this deed and make it beneficial for all of its readers.

Syed Nooruzzuha Barmawar
M-Tech Genetic Engineering
INSERM. France

Umm Amra Noora Jukaku
Graduate in Sharee'ah
College of Usool Al-Deen
University of Sharjah

Introduction of Grand Mufti of Dubai

In The name of Allah, Most Merciful, Most Compassionate.

Praise be to Allah, the Lord, Cherisher and Sustainer of the worlds. The Most Gracious, the Most Merciful; the Master of the Day of Judgment.

All praise is due to Allah, and Allah's Peace and Blessings be upon His Final Messenger, his pure family, his noble companions, and all those who follow them with righteousness and good deeds, until the Day of Reckoning.

Family plays a great role, as it is the first thing we know in our lives and has an everlasting effect on us and on our future.

Islam has laid great emphasis on family life; calling for many points that strengthens and reinforces social relationships, such as: the importance given to the role of the family, treating parents kindly, maintaining good relations with other family members, seeing to the rights and needs of wives and children, etc.

Islam brought with it many needed changes and fruitful reforms into the world. One of the most important social reforms carried out by Islam was the strengthening of the family, the bonds of marriage and the importance of relationships with kith and kin.

In Islamic society, as in many other traditional societies, the family is extended to include grandparents, uncles, aunts and cousins, as well as in-laws.
Many modern cultures and societies have lost the feeling and experience of the extended family. This in turn affects the core

The Blissful Union ©2017 Syed ISBN 978-93-5268-923-1

family itself, leading to the disintegration of family ties and the suffering of children and future generations.

To build up a happy and strong family and a coherent society, Islam emphasizes the importance of the correct man-woman relationship, because they are the pillars of the family.

The marriage tie or contract is described as a strong pledge and a firm covenant.

Allah Almighty says: And how could ye take [part of the dowry] when ye have gone in unto each other and they [the ladies] have taken from you a solemn covenant? Al-Quran (4:21).
Marriage is an important part of the religion, as the Messenger (ﷺ) said, "Marriage is half of the religion"[1].

The marriage contract, when done according to the Islamic rules, legitimizes the physical acts within marriage, protects the rights of both spouses, and safeguards the rights of their children.

---

[1] This hadith is reported by al-Haakim (2/161), at-Tabraani (1/162/1) and by al-Bayhaqi. It is weak due to number of reasons: 1) The chain of this hadith is disconnected, because Abdurrahman bin Zayd bin Aslam is not a Tabiee. He died in 182 H. 2) Abdurrahman bin Zayd is Kadhab and he used to fabricate hadith. Imam Jawzjani called him Kadhab in his book Ahwaal ar-Rijaal page 131. Imam Haakim said: he narrated fabricated ahadith from his father (Al-Madkhal ila as-Saheeh page 154). 3) Another narrator in this chain is Zuhayr bin Muhammad. He is Thiqah but there is Jarh mufassar on him that narrations of people of Shaam from him are daeef. Thus this chain is extremely weak.

The supporting chain of this hadith is present in al-Awsat of at-tabraani (1/162) In this chain there is 1) Yazeed ar-Riqaashi. He is munkarul hadith and extremely weak 2) Another narrator in this chain is Jabir bin Yazeed. He is Kadhab (liar) Imam Yahya bin Ma'een called him Kadhab (Tareekh Yahya bin Maeen 1/210,216) Thus this hadith is extremely weak. Shaykh al-Albani fell into mistake in declaring this hadith to be Hasan in as-Saheehah no.625. Shaykh Ibn Baaz declared it weak in Fataawa Noor ala-al-darb 20/43 and Hafidh Ibn Hajr declared it extremely weak in Al-Kaafi al-Shaaf no.201. [Syed Nooruzzuha]

Basis for family life:
In Islam, family life and marital relationships should be based on three main basics:

- Tranquility, trust, mutual understanding
- Love and intimacy
- And mercy

Allah Almighty says: And among His Signs is this, that He created for you mates from among yourselves, that ye may dwell in tranquility with them, and He has put love and mercy between you, verily in that are Signs for those who reflect. Al-Quran (30:21).

This verse stresses the need for men and women to live in mutual love and respect in order to create an atmosphere of peace for the healthy growth of the family. These three essentials: tranquility, love and mercy need the participation and willingness of both partners in order to be achieved. Tranquility is the basis for the general atmosphere of the house. Tranquility means peace and relaxation, and this can be reached when the family life is based on mutual trust and understanding. Love is the basis for intimate relationships and emotional dealings within the family.

Love needs to be made and maintained. It does not come from nothing, as some people think.
We usually hear the phrase: "love at the first sight". Such love is rare and mostly, it is an exhausting fantasy rather than the real healthy emotion that can be developed, maintained and sustained.

To succeed, love needs the participation of both parties. It needs their words and actions, their sharing of emotions, and their giving and sacrifices for the sake of this great life experience.

Islam calls for the relationship between husband and wife to be the most intimate. The Holy Quran has described this intimate relationship so beautifully when it said that husband and wife are garments for each other.

Allah Almighty says: They [your wives] are raiment for you and ye are raiment for them. Al-Quran (2:187).

Islam prohibits adultery and marital infidelity and that is why Islam teaches and encourages both husband and wife to satisfy the needs of each other. Fulfilling each other's needs and desires is clearly stated in the Al-Quran;

Allah Almighty says:
It is made lawful for you to go unto your wives [to have intimate relation] on the night of the fast. They are raiment for you and ye are raiment for them. Al-Quran (2:187).

This verse is pointing both spouses to meet each other's physical needs and fulfill each other's desires.

Islam encourages the physical side of a marital relationship and treats it as a form of righteousness and obedience to Allah Almighty. This relationship is a form of charity as described by the Messenger(ﷺ), and there is reward for it just like for other good deeds.

The third basis for family life in Islam is 'Mercy'.

Mercy is the basis for dealings and interactions within the family. Mercy is an important part of the religion of Islam, as it calls upon all Muslims to show, practice and extend this mercy towards all people and creatures. Obviously, the family deserves the best part of that merciful way of life.

Some people show mercy to strangers, but deal harshly with their own families, which is ironic and insincere. If they were truly merciful, their family would be first to notice, feel and experience that mercy.

That is why The Messenger (ﷺ) said: "The best of you is those who are best to their family."[2]

Therefore, in Islam, husband and wife should live together in honor and harmony, in trust and mutual understanding, in love and affection, and thereby make home a place of peace and tranquility. Both should respect and complement each other.

Every Muslim family should aspire to have a homogenous happy family that is looked up to as a great model, as Allah Almighty taught us to pray and say: {Our Lord! Grant unto us wives and offspring who will be the comfort of [our] eyes. Al-Quran (25:74). In Islam, both husband and wife have certain rights and duties. These rights and duties are not distributed as 50-50, but according to the abilities and responsibilities of each one in the best, just and fair way, and in accordance with their nature.

There are many obligations on the husband, such as: supporting one's family and paying the dowry of one's wife. Generally, the husband should also provide his family with their needs; proper shelter, clothing, food, health and education, depending on his ability. In exchange, the wife should care for her family and husband's needs, having his

---

[2] It is the authentic hadith reported in Sunan ad-Darimi no. 2306, Sunan Ibn Majah no. 1977, Jaami at-Tirmidhi no. 3895, Musnad al-Bazzar no. 984, Musnad Abee Ya'la no. 5924, Saheeh Ibn Hibban no. 4177, Sharh Mushkil al-Athaar no.2523, Mu'jam al-Awsat at-Tabraanee no. 6145 , Mu'jam al-Kabeer at-Tabraanee no. 853 and Sunan al-Kubra al-Bayhaqi no. 15699.

children and raising them, protecting the property, and upholding the honor, as best as she can. It is the duty of husbands to spend on their families, and men are encouraged to do that and promised great rewards for it.
The Messenger (ﷺ) said: "The best money a man spends is the money he spends on his family".[3]

Treating wives with kindness is part of the faith, as the Messenger (ﷺ) said: "The most perfect in faith amongst believers is he who is best in manner and kindest to his wife."[4]

Muslims are also required to uphold blood relations by visiting their relatives and clearing family feuds, by remaining in touch with one another and supporting one another.

Your family is more important than extra worship. Those who would spend their lives only in worship, forsaking their families are also not practicing moderation or piety. As The Messenger (ﷺ) said: "Your Lord has a right on you, your self has a right on you, and your family has a right on you; so give each party it's well deserved right"[5]

Polygamy in Islam:
As we all know, Islam is the complete code of life, with rules and regulations to accommodate all people, times, races and places. It accommodates for even the most extreme of circumstances, which can also apply to the rules of marriage.

[3] It is the authentic hadith reported in Saheeh Muslim no. 38 , Sunan Ibn Majah no. 2760, Jaami at-Tirmidhi no. 1966 and Sunan al-Kubra Nasa'ee no. 9138.

[4] It is the authentic hadith reported in Sunan Ibn Majah no. 1977, Jaami at-Tirmidhi no. 3895, Musnad Abee Ya'la no. 5924, Saheeh Ibn Hibban no. 4177 and other books.

[5] It is reported in Saheeh al-Bukhari no. 1967, Saheeh Ibn Khuzaymah no. 2144.

There are situations when the partners might not be compatible in all parts of the relationship, physically or otherwise. There are also social considerations such as severe under population and times of war.

One of the ways in Islam to solve such problems is allowing the husband to marry more than one wife, provided he fulfills the very important and very strict condition: to treat them with justice and fairness.

Allah Almighty says: {If ye fear that ye shall not be able to deal justly with the orphans, then marry women of your choice, two or three or four; but if ye fear that ye shall not be able to deal justly (with them), then [marry] only one. Al-Quran (4:3).

If the man knows he cannot treat the wives fairly, and he must consider this very carefully, then it is forbidden for him to marry another wife. There are many required aspects of justice towards the wives. The main aspects are spending [money], clothing, housing and nighttime stay. Therefore, the man must be fair between his wives, dividing times, socializing and showing intimacy. He is not allowed to spend more time with one wife than the other. The husband should try to be as fair as possible. It is recommended that the husband be fair even with kisses and intimate relationships.

The Prophet (ﷺ) warned the husband who does not treat his wives fairly will meet severe punishment in the Hereafter. Polygamy is a more restricting and difficult choice for a husband than monogamy; as he will need to be more careful with his time, gifts, showing affections, traveling, spending and nighttime stay. Polygamy is not actively encouraged in Islam, and is not widely practiced by Muslims.

Divorce and *Khul'*:
The marriage tie is a firm covenant. That is why divorce is considered the most abhorrent of all permitted things.

But life is not perfect, and people are different.

The Quran instructs that reconciliation should be encouraged between husband and wife if a dispute occurs between them to avoid the break up of the family and separation of the children. However, a time may come, when a partner cannot trust the other partner and then they may not be suitable for each other. Marriage ties can be separated for a specific reason or for more general complaints by both the man and the woman. The marriage contract can end by one of the following: death, divorce, separation, *khul'* [conditional divorce], invalidity or breaking of marriage contract etc.

The man can end it by divorce and the woman can end it by *khul'*, more details on that later on. But I must repeat; divorce is considered the most abhorrent of all permitted things. The divorce becomes impermissible if one is sure it is going to lead to bad consequences such as the wasting of children and extreme hurt to the wife.

In Islam, divorce is supposed to be a wise and healthy solution for the benefit of both partners, carried out with kindness and good treatment as Allah Almighty ordered.

The couple is given two separate chances of returning after a declaration of divorce before the last and final divorce is enforced. Divorce is perceived to be initiated by the man in Islam, but ending the marriage can also be initiated by the wife. This is called *Khul'*.

Khul' can be explained as a wife-initiated conditioned divorce or separation. It is allowed in Islam, for Allah Almighty says: {A divorce is only permissible twice: after that the parties should either hold together on equitable terms or separate with kindness. It is not lawful for you (men) to take back any of your gifts (from your wives) except when both parties fear that they would be unable to keep the limits ordained by Allah. If ye (judges) do indeed fear that they would be unable to keep the limits ordained by Allah there is no blame on either of them if she give something for her freedom (what she gives up to become free thereby). These are the limits ordained by Allah; so do not transgress them. If any do transgress the limits ordained by Allah such persons wrong (themselves as well as others)} [Al-Quran (2:229).

The phrase: {give something for her freedom} refers to the wife initiated divorce or *Khul'*. When the husband is not doing his duties or does not give the wife her rights, and also when the wife does not want to live with the husband any more, she can file a case for separation from her husband and returns to him the dowry he gave to her for marriage.

Habibah bint Abdullah the wife of Thabit bin Qays came to the Prophet (ﷺ)and she said, "O Messenger of Allah (ﷺ)! I do not criticize his religion or mannerism. But I hate committing *Kufr* in Islam (by ignoring his rights on her)." Allah's Messenger said: "Will you give him back his garden?" She said, "Yes." Allah's Messenger said to him: "Take back the garden and divorce her once."[6]

Although *Khul'* is initiated by the wife, the actual separation is given by the husband, except in some cases when the husband

---

[6] It is the authentic hadith reported in Saheeh al-Bukhari no. 5273, Musnad Ahmad no. 16095 , Sunan Ibn Majah no. 2056 and other books.

is obstinate and refuses to grant her divorce, then the judge interferes to either conciliate or separate. Muslim parents are responsible for the welfare of the whole family.
The Prophet (ﷺ) said: "Each one of you is a supervisor, and each one of you is responsible for those that he supervises;" and he said: "a husband is the supervisor of his family and he is responsible for those he supervises". The woman also has her share of responsibilities, as the Messenger (ﷺ) said: "A woman is the supervisor of her husband's household and she is responsible for those that she supervises".

I wish you all success and happiness in this world and in the hereafter. We pray to Allah Almighty to grant us good families and offspring, and make us good for them and make them good to us, Amen. We pray to Allah Almighty to make us happy and content, moderate and balanced, inside and outside, and in all aspects of our life, and grant us good things in this world and good things in the hereafter, and save us from the torment of the fire. Amen. We pray to Allah Almighty to guide us to His divine Truth and make us good to ourselves, to our children and family, to our neighbors and society, and then to all humanity. Amen.
Wa Asalm Aliakum
Peace be upon you and the Mercy of Allah and His grace!

Dr. Mohammed Eyada Al-kobaisi
Grand Mufti, Islamic Affairs, Dubai.
15/10/2016

The Blissful Union ©2017 Syed ISBN 978-93-5268-923-1

Introduction

All Praise is due to Allah, we praise Him, seek His aid and His Forgiveness. We seek refuge in Allah from the evils of our souls and the evils of our actions. Whomsoever Allah guides there is none to misguide and whomsoever Allah misguides there is none to guide. I bear witness that there is none worthy of worship except Allah, alone, without any partners and I bear witness that Muhammad is His servant and messenger.

يَـٰٓأَيُّهَا ٱلَّذِينَ ءَامَنُوا۟ ٱتَّقُوا۟ ٱللَّهَ حَقَّ تُقَاتِهِۦ وَلَا تَمُوتُنَّ إِلَّا وَأَنتُم مُّسْلِمُونَ

"O you who believe! Fear Allah as He should be feared, and die not except in a state of Islam (as Muslims) with complete submission to Allah." Al-Quran (3:102)

يَـٰٓأَيُّهَا ٱلنَّاسُ ٱتَّقُوا۟ رَبَّكُمُ ٱلَّذِى خَلَقَكُم مِّن نَّفْسٍ وَٰحِدَةٍ وَخَلَقَ مِنْهَا زَوْجَهَا وَبَثَّ
مِنْهُمَا رِجَالًا كَثِيرًا وَنِسَآءً ۚ وَٱتَّقُوا۟ ٱللَّهَ ٱلَّذِى تَسَآءَلُونَ بِهِۦ وَٱلْأَرْحَامَ ۚ إِنَّ ٱللَّهَ كَانَ
عَلَيْكُمْ رَقِيبًا

"O mankind! Be dutiful to your Lord, Who created you from a single person (Adam),and from him (Adam) He created his wife, and from them both He created many men and women and fear Allah through Whom you demand your mutual (rights), and (do not cut the relations of) the wombs (kinship). Surely, Allah is Ever an All-Watcher over you." Al-Quran (4:1)

يَـٰٓأَيُّهَا ٱلَّذِينَ ءَامَنُوا۟ ٱتَّقُوا۟ ٱللَّهَ وَقُولُوا۟ قَوْلًا سَدِيدًا . يُصْلِحْ لَكُمْ أَعْمَـٰلَكُمْ وَيَغْفِرْ
لَكُمْ ذُنُوبَكُمْ ۗ وَمَن يُطِعِ ٱللَّهَ وَرَسُولَهُۥ فَقَدْ فَازَ فَوْزًا عَظِيمًا

"O you who believe! Keep your duty to Allah and fear Him, and speak (always) the truth. He will direct you to do righteous

The Blissful Union ©2017 Syed ISBN 978-93-5268-923-1

good deeds and will forgive your sins. And whosoever obeys Allah and His Messenger, he has indeed achieved a great achievement (i.e. he will be saved from the Hell-fire and made to enter Paradise)." Al-Quran (33:70-71)

To proceed, verily the best speech is the Book of Allah and the best of guidance is the guidance of Muhammad (ﷺ). And the worst of affairs are the newly invented matters, every newly-invented matter is an innovation, every innovation is misguidance and all misguidance is in the Hellfire.

Islam is the religion which was given to Adam, the first man and the first prophet of Allah, and it was the religion of all the prophets sent by Allah to mankind. Islam is a complete way of life for the human being.

Allah says in Al-Quran (5:3):

ٱلْيَوْمَ أَكْمَلْتُ لَكُمْ دِينَكُمْ وَأَتْمَمْتُ عَلَيْكُمْ نِعْمَتِى وَرَضِيتُ لَكُمُ ٱلْإِسْلَـٰمَ دِينًا

This day have I perfected your religion for you, completed my favor upon you, and have chosen for you Islam as your religion.

Islam provides guidance in every aspect of life, from purity and prayer to business transactions, family and inheritance. It takes into account all of mankind's needs: spiritual, emotional and physical.
It is reported in *Saheeh Muslim* no. 262:

عَنْ سَلْمَانَ، قَالَ قِيلَ لَهُ قَدْ عَلَّمَكُمْ نَبِيُّكُمْ صلى الله عليه وسلم كُلَّ شَىْءٍ حَتَّى
الْخِرَاءَةَ . قَالَ فَقَالَ أَجَلْ لَقَدْ نَهَانَا أَنْ نَسْتَقْبِلَ الْقِبْلَةَ لِغَائِطٍ أَوْ بَوْلٍ أَوْ أَنْ

The Blissful Union ©2017 Syed ISBN 978-93-5268-923-1

نَسْتَنْجِيَ بِالْيَمِينِ أَوْ أَنْ نَسْتَنْجِيَ بِأَقَلَّ مِنْ ثَلاَثَةِ أَحْجَارٍ أَوْ أَنْ نَسْتَنْجِيَ بِرَجِيعٍ أَوْ بِعَظْمٍ

Salman reported that it was said to him: Your Prophet(ﷺ) teaches you about everything, even about excrement. He replied: Yes, he has forbidden us to face the Qibla at the time of excretion or urination, or cleansing with right hand or with less than three pebbles, or with dung or bone.

Accordingly, Islam does not neglect the subject of marriage and intimacy, rather Islam provides guidelines regarding it. Scholars of *hadith* such as Imam Al-Bukhari, Imam Abu Dawood and many others have dedicated books in their collection of *ahadith* as *"Kitab an-Nikah"* (Book of marriage) collecting narrations from Prophet(ﷺ) on subject of marriage and intimacy. Similarly scholars of *Fiqh* (Jurisprudence) have written books on this subject. It recognizes the physical and emotional needs of a man and a woman. Due to this reason Allah has laid down the guidelines to achieve marital bliss. After the creation of Adam, Allah created Hawwa which indicates the importance of marriage and relationship between husband and wife.

In this *Tech-savvy* generation it is extremely important to present Islamic teachings on the subjects of marriage, love and intimacy, without which Muslims would be left to study the matter from un-Islamic sources and fall into misguidance. If one does not gain access to the right sources to study from about marriage and intimacy there are high chances that they might resort to erotic books to educate themselves about intimate relations which will cause them to have farce ideologies about sex and their spouse in general. Educating oneself correctly about marriage can block many trials one can face in married life.

We ask Allah to preserve Muslim *Ummah* from falling into misguidance and the tribulations that come with it.

The Blissful Union ©2017 Syed ISBN 978-93-5268-923-1

Why Marry?

This question may arise in many young minds today, those who try to run away from the idea of marriage. Media and society have placed such a negative influence on our youth that the whole concept of marriage has been distorted and portrayed as something detestable. They are manipulated into thinking that love only exists outside of marriage in *Haram* relationships where the opposite genders interact in the most inappropriate manner and they have started to believe that once a person gets married, his or her life comes to an end. Running away from responsibilities would be another reason why someone would refuse marriage altogether. Such people miss out on seeing the tremendous benefits marriage brings in peoples lives.

Marriage makes an incomplete human being a complete one. It is a life-long commitment that restrains self-centeredness, self-indulgence and self-gratification. It is supposed to take a person out of the hectic lifestyle that one is in and place him or her in an organized environment giving them a path to follow in life and a shoulder to lean on. It also provides an opportunity to grow in selflessness as you serve your spouse and children. It is more than a physical union; it is also an emotional union. The bond of marriage gives us the support to defeat that temptation by engaging in deep, satisfying love; a love that gives to, and receives from, our mate physically and emotionally. There are many who have regained emotional and physical health after getting married due to the love, support and companionship they receive from their spouse.

Marriage also helps oneself to gain a higher level of *Taqwa* by protecting them from sin which otherwise would be difficult to achieve while being single.

Allah states in Al-Quran (30:21):

وَمِنْ ءَايَـٰتِهِۦٓ أَنْ خَلَقَ لَكُم مِّنْ أَنفُسِكُمْ أَزْوَٰجًا لِّتَسْكُنُوٓا۟ إِلَيْهَا وَجَعَلَ بَيْنَكُم مَّوَدَّةً وَرَحْمَةً ۚ إِنَّ فِى ذَٰلِكَ لَـَٔايَـٰتٍ لِّقَوْمٍ يَتَفَكَّرُونَ

"And of His signs is that He created for you from yourselves mates that you may find tranquility in them; and He placed between you affection and mercy. Indeed in that are signs for a people who give thought."

In *Tafseer* of this Ayah, Great *Mufassir* (exegete) from *Tabi'een,* student of companion Anas bin Malik, Imam Qatadah (May Allah be pleased with him) said:

(وَرَحْمَةً) رحمكم بها، فعطف بعضكم بذلك على بعض

"(and mercy- meaning) Allah has bestowed mercy upon you through her (marrying her), therefore, both have affection for each other." This explanation of Imam Qatadah is reported by Imam Ibn Jareer At-Tabari in his *Tafseer* (2/86) with an authentic chain of narration.

Imam Ash-Shawkani said in his *Tafseer Fath Al-Qadeer* (4/253) in explanation of this Ayah:

وَجَعَلَ بَيْنَكُمْ مَوَدَّةً وَرَحْمَةً أَيْ: وِدَادًا وَتَرَاحُمًا بِسَبَبِ عِصْمَةِ النِّكَاحِ يَعْطِفُ بِهِ بَعْضُكُمْ عَلَى بَعْضٍ مِنْ غَيْرِ أَنْ يَكُونَ بَيْنَكُمْ قَبْلَ ذَلِكَ مَعْرِفَةٌ فَضْلًا عَنْ مَوَدَّةٍ وَرَحْمَةٍ

And (Allah) put between you both *Mawaddah* (love) and *Rahmah* (mercy) i.e, sincere affection (closeness) and being merciful towards each other, due to the bondage of *Nikah*, by which both are affectionate towards each other, even though you didn't know each other before. That sincere love and mercy are the fruits (of *Nikah*).

Imam Ibn Majah narrated in his *Sunan* no.1919 with an authentic chain that Messenger of Allah (ﷺ) said:

قَالَ رَسُولُ اللَّهِ ـ صلى الله عليه وسلم ـ " النِّكَاحُ مِنْ سُنَّتِي فَمَنْ لَمْ يَعْمَلْ
بِسُنَّتِي فَلَيْسَ مِنِّي وَتَزَوَّجُوا فَإِنِّي مُكَاثِرٌ بِكُمُ الأُمَمَ وَمَنْ كَانَ ذَا طَوْلٍ فَلْيَنْكِحْ
وَمَنْ لَمْ يَجِدْ فَعَلَيْهِ بِالصِّيَامِ فَإِنَّ الصَّوْمَ لَهُ وِجَاءٌ " .

"Marriage is part of my sunnah, and whoever does not follow my sunnah has nothing to do with me. Get married, for I will boast of your great numbers before the nations. Whoever has the means, let him get married, and whoever does not, then he should fast for it will diminish his desire."

The Blissful Union ©2017 Syed ISBN 978-93-5268-923-1

Marriage is a mutual concealment

Allah says in Al-Quran (2:187):

هُنَّ لِبَاسٌ لَّكُمْ وَأَنتُمْ لِبَاسٌ لَّهُنَّ

"They are *Libas* [i.e. body cover, screen or garment] for you and you are the same for them."

Famous scholar of *Tafseer* from *Tabi'een*, Imam Mujahid (student of the companion Ibn Abbas) explained this Ayah as reported by Ibn Jareer in his *Tafseer* (3/492) no.2931 with an authentic chain:

هن لباس لكم وأنتم لباسٌ لهن"، يقول: سكنٌ لهن"

They (your wives) are garments for you and you are garments for them (meaning: you find comfort and tranquility in them, you enjoy the pleasure of living with them).

Another scholar of *Tafseer* from *Tabi'een* Imam Qatadah explained the above *Ayah* as reported by Ibn Jareer in his *Tafseer* (3/492) no.2930 with an authentic chain:

هُنّ سكنٌ لكم، وأنتم سكنٌ لهنّ"

"They (your wives) are comfort for you, and you are comfort for them (i.e. you enjoy the pleasure of living with them)."

Imam al-Qurtubi explained this *Ayah* in his *Tafseer* (2/316) :

كُلٌّ وَاحِدٌ مِنْهُمَا سِتْرًا لِصَاحِبِهِ عَمَّا لَا يَحِلُّ

"Each one of them is a protection for their spouse from that which is impermissible (just like garments protect person from nakedness)."

Clothing is a means by which one beautifies oneself. Just like one would be incomplete and feel odd while naked and without clothing, similarly, a person who is not married is incomplete and would feel like something is missing in their life. Marriage completes a person in every sense and beautifies them like clothing beautifies them. Marriage, like clothing, is an essential part of a person's life.

The Blissful Union ©2017 Syed ISBN 978-93-5268-923-1

Marriage vs Live-in relationship

The west portrays that marital bliss can only be obtained if two people meet with no restrictions prior to marriage. This allows both of them to meet each other, live together and have illicit sexual relations, all "to get to know each other better".

This is so they can get to learn the other person's behavioral traits and personality so that they can be more compatible with each other in order to make the relationship more lasting. However, this idea that has sadly seeped into the Muslim world as well, is a big fallacy.

This trial of live-in relationships also has adverse effects on families and society. Neither of the two can trust each other, as before marriage, couples put up an act for each other so they can impress their partner. Such relationships tend to be very fragile since it is not based on any solid foundation like marriage where both sign a contract.

Also, experience is enough evidence that women tend to suffer more in live-in relationships. Since it is an easy way out in live-in relationships, anything from a small fight, disagreement, or a misplaced question can see either of the partners walking out of the relationship. Since, by nature, women are emotional, it becomes difficult for them to find a good and understanding spouse after being in a live-in relationship with someone else. Someone might say that "if one man leaves me I will find another one". This statement and act doesn't complement the nature of women and in fact, constantly changing partners has detrimental effects on the confidence of women and their personality in general. She will harbour feelings of great insecurity and a rise in fears with regard to

The Blissful Union ©2017 Syed ISBN 978-93-5268-923-1

relationships, making her unable to be stable in any other relationship.

Islam, however, gives a completely different perspective on marriage and the reason why marriage has been prescribed by the Almighty.

Allah states in Al-Quran (30:21):

وَمِنْ ءَايَـٰتِهِۦٓ أَنْ خَلَقَ لَكُم مِّنْ أَنفُسِكُمْ أَزْوَٰجًا لِّتَسْكُنُوٓا۟ إِلَيْهَا وَجَعَلَ بَيْنَكُم مَّوَدَّةً
وَرَحْمَةً ۚ إِنَّ فِى ذَٰلِكَ لَـَٔايَـٰتٍ لِّقَوْمٍ يَتَفَكَّرُونَ

"And of His signs is that He created for you from yourselves mates that you may find tranquility in them; and He placed between you affection and mercy. Indeed in that are signs for a people who give thought."

Allah mentions that this beautiful relationship between two souls bound by a contract is a sign from the many signs of Allah. A sign from Allah, like the sun, moon, stars, day and night etc., is something that a believer ponders upon to become closer to his lord. Similarly, it is a sign from Him that He has created for each a mate from within themselves, the sole purpose being that they may find tranquility in each other. Whoever fulfills this in the manner Allah has prescribed then surely Allah will place between them affection and mercy - the very essence that many marriages today lack. This is only because we do not follow the path that Allah has laid down for us regarding marriage. Rather, we try to emulate what is fed to us through the media and what the western society follows and instead our marriages head towards unpleasant consequences and many a time end up in divorce. While Allah says that marriage is so that we can find peace and tranquility within the constitution, with two spouses giving each other love, showing mercy, affection and kindness, taking care of each others' needs, and fulfilling the rights of one another. This can only be achieved if both spouses fear Allah and do for each other to attain closeness and the pleasure of Allah. Only the people who give it a thought would truly understand and comprehend these signs that are mentioned in the *Ayah*.

So, marriage is such a bond that it gives both male and female tranquility and companionship. A married person, if married to the right person, feels a sense of security and comfort which otherwise wouldn't be felt while he or she is single.

The Blissful Union ©2017 Syed ISBN 978-93-5268-923-1

The earlier the better

Marriage helps a person channel their desires in a lawful manner while gaining the reward for it from the Almighty, and it is better that a person seeks to get married at young age. "Why get married early?" some may ask. We say…Why not?? The most important and also exciting time of life is the age of youth. So wouldn't we want our other half to be part of this time in our life, experiencing many firsts, sharing and living the ups and downs of life, and growing together? Also, when a person is young they adjust better. They are more tolerant towards another person which gives higher chances for the marriage to survive, rather than reaching an age where one has already developed a fixed mindset and are used to having things a certain way, then get married to someone being unable to compromise because they feel that they cannot change their ideology and the way they are living, which in turn complicates many matters. Even if they are older, it is highly recommended that they get married, but the point here is that it would take them much more time to adapt than if they would have gotten married earlier. Moreover, getting married early has tremendous benefits for the person as the individual will be saved from a lot of *fitnah* that they might fall into later on if they stay single.

Imam al-Bukhari narrates in his *Saheeh*, in *Book of Nikah*, no. 5066

قَالَ عَبْدُ اللَّهِ كُنَّا مَعَ النَّبِيِّ صلى الله عليه وسلم شَبَابًا لاَ نَجِدُ شَيْئًا فَقَالَ
لَنَا رَسُولُ اللَّهِ صلى الله عليه وسلم " يَا مَعْشَرَ الشَّبَابِ مَنِ اسْتَطَاعَ
الْبَاءَةَ فَلْيَتَزَوَّجْ، فَإِنَّهُ أَغَضُّ لِلْبَصَرِ، وَأَحْصَنُ لِلْفَرْجِ، وَمَنْ لَمْ يَسْتَطِعْ فَعَلَيْهِ
بِالصَّوْمِ، فَإِنَّهُ لَهُ وِجَاءٌ "

“Narrated Abdullah: We were with the Prophet (ﷺ) while we were young and had no wealth whatever. So Allah's Messenger (ﷺ) said, "O young people! Whoever among you can marry, should marry, because it helps him lower his gaze and guard his modesty (i.e. his private parts from committing illegal sexual intercourse etc.), and whoever is not able to marry, should fast, as fasting diminishes his sexual power.”

The Prophet (ﷺ) gave a great advice for the youth mentioning that marriage saves one from great tribulations because it helps us to lower our gaze, which in turn protects us from falling into committing that which is forbidden. One of the benefits of marrying at an early age is that you will have an easier time having kids, and there are more chances that your kids will be healthy and you will be able to keep up with them better.

Marry at a young age- a lesson

A true story comes to mind that took place in our hometown which shows the importance of marriage and getting married early.

It is a story of a girl who was brought up in a reputed and religious family where both her parents were religiously devoted, and her father was well known in many religious organizations throughout India.The girl had reached the age of maturity, around 18 years old, and wanted to get married but she was unable to communicate this to her parents. Unable to fulfill her desires in a lawful manner, she started looking for unlawful means and fell into *Haram* (illicit) relationships. A couple of days later, she was caught with a man and her parents were informed, upon which they reprimanded her vehemently. Her reputation was soiled amongst the people of the town which made it very difficult to find a suitable spouse for her.

Her parents strictly blocked all the means of communication for her. Yet again, as the time passed, she was found repeating the same thing with another man. They rebuked her even more strongly this time and upon asking why she was doing such disgraceful acts, she cried and screamed saying: “Then why don't you get me married?” Thereafter, her parents decided to send her to a religious school where she was confined within a small room, not allowed to go out anywhere at all except to the school itself. She had to do all her work by herself. Some time passed and she started feeling very ill, upon which her parents decided to take her back home. After her illness was treated, she fell back into the same sins she was committing, this time with a boy much younger than herself with whom she ran away. Upon finding out this time, her parents at last decided to get her married but it was very difficult to find her a spouse, since the whole town knew her

The Blissful Union ©2017 Syed ISBN 978-93-5268-923-1

story. Finally, they found a boy who was of the same nature and had chosen *Haram* means to fulfill his desires. They paid him a large sum of money to marry their daughter, to which he agreed, and they married her to him. After getting married, the couple reformed themselves and changed completely and are now living happy married life.

This is one of the many incidents I have narrated here to show the significance of marriage and how getting married early has so many benefits to the individuals and the society as a whole as it wards off many evils.

The Blissful Union ©2017 Syed ISBN 978-93-5268-923-1

Researches on marrying early

According to a research article by Ewen Callaway published in 2012 in a journal *Nature*: "Children of older fathers have increased risks for several physical and mental disorders compared to children of younger fathers. And it is also scientifically established that it's easier to conceive when you and your wife are younger."

According to a demographic research done by Evelyn Lehrer and Yu Chen, published in *Journal of Population Sciences*, you are more likely to marry a true peer and someone whom you have lots in common with if you marry in your 20s as opposed to marrying later.
Dr. Meg Jay, author of *The Defining Decade: Why Your Twenties Matter--And How to Make the Most of Them Now* says: "Even though searching may help you find a better partner, the pool of available singles shallows over time, perhaps in more ways than one."

Another research done by Norval Glenn and team, published in *Journal of Social Science Research* in 2010, showed, couples who married at a young age were more likely to describe their marriage as "very happy" than couples who got married in other age brackets. The researchers conclude that the reason marital satisfaction declines after the age of 25 is that spouses that get married older often feel like they are "settling" with a less-than-ideal marriage partner.

This is not only proven by research but it is also known through experience and we are witness to this that the older a person gets, the more difficult it becomes for them to find a suitable spouse as their choices become narrower. There are many who have compromised on important matters because they have grown older unable to find someone and needed to get married. So they get married to someone due to this need and feel discontented in many issues relating to their spouse. It is even more so for those who have compromised religion for the same reason leading into dreadful marriages.

Early marriage helps you reach your academic and career goals by providing focus and stability. According to a study published by W. Bradford Wilcox and Robert I. Lerman in October 2014, married men in their 20s are more focused and work harder than their single peers.

A thin line distinguishing Infatuation, Passionate love & True love...

Infatuation

"I am in love with him", "I really love her", we often hear these words from our friends and relatives. There are so many people who are convinced that they are in love with someone just because they can't stop thinking about them. The truth however is, most of the time the emotion that comes with really liking someone is not love, it's infatuation. Infatuation is delusional, and many a times blinds the individual from seeing reality. It makes one act irrationally or go crazy. In every age-group, especially in that of the teenage and young adulthood, this phenomenon of so-called 'love' creates waves but in most cases it's delusional infatuation.

If we look at college life, workplace, TV shows, movies, novels etc., we learn that love seems to be on everyone's mind. Satan may cause each one to see in the other, attributes that cause them to become infatuated, which has a negative impact on their worldly and religious affairs. Satan encourages people to commit *Haram* (impermissible) actions and makes people's deeds appear attractive to them, approaching each person in a different manner. Infatuation can make a person lose their mind and do things that are unreasonable and sometimes lead to a person's destruction, depending on the extent to which they can go. For example: in an instance where a muslim girl thinks she is in love with a non muslim man, her infatuation for him may take her to the point where she feels she will not be able to live without him, which could lead her to take inappropriate steps such as leaving her parents, her home and even her religion.

But since these feelings are held in a person's heart only temporarily, infatuation will definitely leave their mind once they find someone better than the one they previously liked.

Allah says in Al-Quran (24:21):

يَـٰٓأَيُّهَا ٱلَّذِينَ ءَامَنُوا۟ لَا تَتَّبِعُوا۟ خُطُوَٰتِ ٱلشَّيْطَـٰنِ ۚ وَمَن يَتَّبِعْ خُطُوَٰتِ ٱلشَّيْطَـٰنِ فَإِنَّهُۥ يَأْمُرُ بِٱلْفَحْشَآءِ وَٱلْمُنكَرِ

"O you who believe! Follow not the footsteps of Satan. And whosoever follows the footsteps of Satan, then, verily he commands *Al-Fahsha* [i.e., to commit indecency (illegal sexual intercourse etc.)], and *Al-Munkar* [disbelief and polytheism (i.e. to do evil and wicked deeds; to speak or to do what is forbidden in Islam, etc.)]."

Islam blocks the avenues to anything that even leads one closer to committing forbidden acts and there are many commandments and prohibitions we find in the Quran. It blocks all ways leading to temptation.

Islam forbids women to speak in a soft voice.

Allah says in Al-Quran (33:32):

إِنِ ٱتَّقَيْتُنَّ فَلَا تَخْضَعْنَ بِٱلْقَوْلِ فَيَطْمَعَ ٱلَّذِى فِى قَلْبِهِۦ مَرَضٌ وَقُلْنَ قَوْلًا مَّعْرُوفًا

"If you keep your duty (to Allah), then be not soft in speech, lest he in whose heart is a disease (of hypocrisy, or evil desire for adultery etc.) should be moved with desire, but speak in an honorable manner."

Islamic prohibits men to look at women with lustful eyes

Allah says in Al-Quran (24:30):

قُل لِّلْمُؤْمِنِينَ يَغُضُّواْ مِنْ أَبْصَـٰرِهِمْ

"Tell the believing men to lower their gaze."

Islam also prohibits being alone with woman. Messenger of Allah said in an authentic *hadith* reported by Imam Tirmidhi in his *Jaami* no. 1171

يَخْلُوَنَّ رَجُلٌ بِامْرَأَةٍ إِلَّا كَانَ ثَالِثَهُمَا الشَّيْطَانُ

"No man is alone with a woman but the Satan is the third one present."

Islam commands modesty and piety in every aspect in one's life, which if lacking in a person, can cause them to commit acts of immorality of all types. The attribute of immodesty coupled with infatuation can bring about more harmful consequences in the society as a whole. Imagine how society would be where couples would follow these commandments, then all marriages would be built on perfect trust and many of the trials would reduce, but this is only something we could imagine because not everyone accepts the truth and Allah is sought for refuge.

We will narrate here two such cases of infatuation to show how people react when it comes to such feelings yet when they are taken out of that situation come back to normal as if nothing had happened in the first place.
The first is of a girl, sixteen years old, who was going to school. She met a boy and both were attracted to each other. He came to her and asked her to be his girlfriend and because

of her liking of him she agreed. They started sending each other messages online, followed by long conversations on the phone and it got to the point where they even started meeting each other, secretly and obviously without the knowledge of her parents. Their messages even contained of intimacy. He would wait for her outside her building when it was time for her to go to school and then both would go hang out instead of going to school. This continued for quite some time and like any other relationship things were very rosy in the beginning. As time passed though they started having fights. Not a single phone call would go without a heated argument. Both would decide to ignore each other but then would get back again. Two years passed. Within these years they had even got caught by her parents and her father had even threatened him that he would get him in serious trouble if he didn't leave his daughter alone. The girl upon being reprimanded by her parents still didn't change her ways, instead she would fight back and once when asked by her mother angrily if she will get married to him, she screamed that she definitely will. What is more surprising here, is that when both graduated from school and went their own ways where he moved to another country and she got busy with her university, they both completely forgot about each other. The girl now is happily married. Do you really think this is love? Indeed true love is actually something very different!

The other narrative is of a boy who was extremely infatuated with a girl. He would spend his entire days and nights thinking about her and would feel that he wouldn't be able to live without her. He had even refused to get married thinking that he will only get married to her. If she wouldn't talk to him he would hit his head hard against the wall. Whenever she would message him, he would sit hours concentrating on her words and would even call his friends to interpret her statements and

The Blissful Union ©2017 Syed ISBN 978-93-5268-923-1

what she meant. He would even pray night prayer (*Tahajjud*) making *Dua* so that he can get her. He went so deep into this state of infatuation that if something went wrong he would even go the to the extent of uttering wrong statements about Allah that were *kufr.* When his friends used to try to advise him he would say out in anger that he doesn't need their advice. Some time passed and he started reforming, later he chose another girl for marriage because of her religion. That's when he admitted to his friends that the feelings he had before for the other girl was only infatuation.

Many a time, women due to their emotional nature, are under the impression that since they are in love with a person, they won't be able to live without them, start fancying life with their beloved and when they enter into a new life with this person, the opposite holds to be true. They are mistreated and abused by these men, and in worse case, if he was a disbeliever, because one who is not a believer what character will he display with one who is a believer. Even though this does not happen in all instances and one may argue that many times such marriages work out really well. We say, what guarantee does one hold that after running away against the will of your guardian and leaving your family for this person, that this marriage will survive as you had thought and how can one really trust someone they met a few months or a year or two ago. May Allah guide us and our offspring and protect this nation *(Ummah)* from such great tribulations. May Allah help us be firm on His religion and preserve us and our families from being led astray.

The Blissful Union ©2017 Syed ISBN 978-93-5268-923-1

Passionate love

Passionate love is very different from infatuation. Falling in love can cause havoc on one's body. In passionate love, people feel that their heart races and as if they are on an emotional roller coaster, feeling extremely happy one minute and anxious and sad the next.

Shaykhul Islam Ibn Taymiyyah said in *Majmoo' al-Fataawa* (10/185):

والعشق مرض نفسانى ، وإذا قوي أثَّر فى البدن ، فصار مرضا فى الجسم : إما من أمراض الدماغ ، ولهذا قيل فيه هو مرض وسواسي ، وإما من أمراض البدن كالضعف والنحول ونحو ذلك

"And passionate love is a psychological sickness, and when it becomes strong it affects the body, and becomes sickness in the body, either as diseases of the brain, which are said to be diseases caused by whisperings, or diseases of the body such as weakness, leanness and so on."

Senior Psychologist JoAnn Deak said: "We now know that the chemical changes in parts of the brain, when you're in love, are equal to that of heroin doses or high cocaine doses, so you kind of know — If you have to ask if you're in love, you're not."

According to scientific research paper *"The neural basis of romantic love"* published by Andreas Bartels and Semir Zeki in the year 2000, chemical changes and changes in activity of the brain is observed on those who are in romantic love.

If a man is in love with a woman or if a woman is in deep love with a man, there is no answer to the problem except marriage. This is the cure of love.

Messenger of Allah ﷺ said in an authentic *hadith* reported by Ibn Majah in his *Sunan* no.1847:

لم نرَ للمتحابَّيْن مثل النكاح

"There is nothing like marriage, for two who love one another."

Al-Manaawi said in explanation of this *hadith* in his book *"Faydh-al-Qadeer"*:

إذا نظر رجل لأجنبية وأخذت بمجامع قلبه فنكاحها يورثه مزيد المحبة، كذا ذكر الطيبي، وأفصح منه قول بعض الأكابر المراد أن أعظم الأدوية التي يعالج بها العشق النكاح، فهو علاجه الذي لا يعدل عنه لغيره ما وجد إليه سبيلا

"If a man looks at a lady who is a stranger and she conquers his heart then marrying her will bring about more love, as mentioned by At-Tayyibi, and the statement of some senior ones is more eloquent than his, meaning that the greatest medicine that cures passionate love is *Nikah*, so it is an ultimate cure for it where nothing else matches it."

And if a person is unable to marry someone with whom he is in love with then he should strive and seek cure from this disease. We hope the following points will be a guide on how to get over that person with whom you are in love with.

1) Ask Allah to help you get cured from this disease, increase in performing good deeds and make du'a to Allah to ease your pain and help you to be content. Allah will find a way out for you from this difficulty.

Allah says in Al-Quran (65:2):

وَمَن يَتَّقِ ٱللَّهَ يَجۡعَل لَّهُۥ مَخۡرَجٗا

"And whosoever fears Allah and keeps his duty to Him, He will make a way for him to get out (from every difficulty)."

Messenger of Allah ﷺ said in an authentic *hadith* reported by Imam Tirmidhi in his *Jaami* no.2516:

إذا سألت فاسأل الله ، وإذا استعنت فاستعن بالله ، واعلم أن الأمة لو اجتمعت على أن ينفعوك بشيء ، لم ينفعوك إلا بشيء قد كتبه الله لك ، وإن اجتمعوا على أن يضروك بشيء لم يضروك إلا بشيء قد كتبه الله عليك

"If you ask, then ask Allah; and if you seek help, then seek help from Allah. And know that if the nation were to gather together to benefit you with anything, they would not benefit you except with what Allah had already prescribed for you. And if they were to gather together to harm you with anything, they would not harm you except with what Allah had already prescribed against you."

2) Accept the decree of Allah

When you are not able to marry a person with whom you are madly in love with then it's tempting to dwell on what you did wrong or what you could have done differently. This might seem productive like you can somehow change things by

The Blissful Union ©2017 Syed ISBN 978-93-5268-923-1

rehashing it. Don't do this. Keep reminding yourself that it's a decree from Allah.

Messenger of Allah ﷺ said in an authentic *hadith* reported by Tirmidhi in his *Jaami* no.2396

إنَّ عِظم الجزاء مع عظم البلاء ، وإنَّ الله عز وجل إذا أحب قوماً ابتلاهم ، فمن رضي فله الرضا ، ومن سخط فله السخط

"The greatest reward comes with the greatest trial. When Allah loves people He tests them. Whoever accepts that wins His pleasure but whoever is discontent with that earns His wrath."

Shaykhul Islam Ibn Taymiyyah said in *Majmoo' al-Fataawa* (10/133): "If one is tested with love but he remains chaste and is patient, then he will be rewarded for fearing Allah"

3) Remind yourself that Allah is all-knowing and he has the knowledge of unseen.

Only Allah knows whether or not that person would bring you closer to Him or distract you from the real purpose in life. It is only Allah who knows. Allah says in Al-Quran (2:216):

وَعَسَىٰٓ أَن تَكۡرَهُواْ شَيۡـًٔا وَهُوَ خَيۡرٞ لَّكُمۡۖ وَعَسَىٰٓ أَن تُحِبُّواْ شَيۡـًٔا وَهُوَ شَرّٞ لَّكُمۡۚ وَٱللَّهُ يَعۡلَمُ وَأَنتُمۡ لَا تَعۡلَمُونَ

"And it may be that you dislike a thing which is good for you and that you like a thing which is bad for you. Allah knows but you do not know."

Many a times people are in love with a person and after spending some time with them, getting to know them, they decide they are going to spend their lives with them. But because this person was "putting on an act", after they really start living together within wedlock, they start to see the true side of this person and what they knew about this person before was something completely different. Reality then hits them hard and not only do they come out of this state of love but they start to harbor dislike for this person sometimes turning into sheer hatred. We have seen, for this reason, many marriages failing and breaking apart. Only Allah knows the consequences of any situation and many a times he protects us from falling into what will cause our destruction.

4) Treating one's heart:

One must treat his heart by putting a stop to the effects of this love, and by filling his heart with love of Allah,pondering over *ayaat* of Quran and seeking His help in that. One may study books like *"Diseases of the Hearts and Their Cures"* by Shaykhul Islam Ibn Taymiyyah, *"Disciplining The Soul"* of Imam Ibn Jawzi, *"Spiritual Disease And It's Cure"* by Imam Ibn Qayyim, *"The Tree of Faith"* by Shaykh Abdurrahman bin Nasir As-Saadi etc.

5) Work on fearful thoughts

You may have thoughts like I'll never feel loved again. I'll always feel lonely. I am completely powerless.

Remember words of Allah in Al-Quran (94:6)

إِنَّ مَعَ ٱلْعُسْرِ يُسْرًا

The Blissful Union ©2017 Syed ISBN 978-93-5268-923-1

Verily, along with hardship is relief

All pain passes eventually. You should replace those fearful thoughts with thoughts like: I can't always control what happens to me, but I can control how I respond to it. It will be easier if I help them pass by being mindful and so on.
And we have to understand that Allah is *Al Jabbar* and that He will definitely mend our hearts and cure us of every pain like He has promised.

6) Socialize

Meeting people, friends or relatives, reminds how there is a whole world out there. Allah has enjoined upon us to maintain family relations. Don't get cooped up with your life.

7) Seeking advice from wise people

One should not feel shy to consult intelligent and trustworthy people for advice or consult some doctors and psychologists, because he may find some remedy with them.

8) *Dhikr* : Constant remembrance of Allah

Allah says in Al-Quran (13:28):

أَلَا بِذِكْرِ ٱللَّهِ تَطْمَئِنُّ ٱلْقُلُوبُ

Verily, in the remembrance of Allah do hearts find rest.

True Love: Love for the sake of Allah

While it is natural for spouses to love each other and there is nothing wrong with that, but here we will discuss the type of love which is no doubt the strongest type of love that will be an everlasting bond continued even beyond the realm of this world. It will continue even in the hereafter where those two people who love each other for the sake of their lord are one of the seven people who will find shade on that day where there will be no shade except His shade.

It is mentioned by Imam Al-Bukhari in his *Saheeh* no. 1423

عَنِ النَّبِيِّ صلى الله عليه وسلم قَالَ
وَرَجُلاَنِ تَحَابَّا فِي اللَّهِ اجْتَمَعَا عَلَيْهِ وَتَفَرَّقَا عَلَيْهِ...سَبْعَةٌ يُظِلُّهُمُ اللَّهُ تَعَالَى...
فِي ظِلِّهِ يَوْمَ لاَ ظِلَّ إِلاَّ ظِلُّهُ

The Prophet ﷺ said, "Seven people will be shaded by Allah under His shade on the day when there will be no shade except His. They are:...
Two persons who love each other only for Allah's sake and they meet and part in Allah's cause only...

This kind of love which is the most beautiful and strongest type of bond one can experience is lacking in most marriages today. If both spouses were to really love each other for the sake of Allah building their marriages upon His obedience and staying away from His prohibitions, then this marriage will not only thrive in this world but will even continue its journey to the everlasting abode- Paradise.

Scholar of *hadith*, Shaykh Al-Albani explains price [to be paid] for loving someone for Allah's sake as collected in *Al-Haawi min Fataawaa al-Albaani*, pages. 165-166:

And an explanation of that is that if I really love you for the sake of Allah I would persist in advising you, and you would do the same. Persevering in advising one another is very rare between those who claim to love each other, this love might have some sincerity in it, but it is not complete, because we try to make an allowance for the other, afraid that the other person will become angry, that he will flee … and so on.

It is in light of this that [you can see that] the cost of loving someone for the sake of Allah is that each person shows sincerity towards the other by advising him, always and forever telling him to do good and preventing him from bad—he is more constant in advising him than that person's own shadow is close—for this reason it has been authentically reported that when parting from one another, one of the habits of the Companions was that one of them would read to the other, "By Time! Indeed, mankind is in loss. Except for those who have believed and done righteous deeds and advised each other to truth and advised each other to patience." Al-Quran (103:1-3)*[7]

On the other hand, we see in our times a sad state of affairs, where marriages are full of disagreements and fall apart due to this very sole reason that they are based on temporary and materialistic affairs. When one marries only for reasons like beauty or wealth, the very moment they see these things deteriorate, they immediately walk away from the relationship and try to find something better than this. While those who

---

[7] Taken from translation of Ahmed Abu Turaab

marry based on *Deen* and love each other for the sake of Allah will always overlook each other's faults and accept their shortcomings trying and working around them together as one. They know this life is not everlasting and the people are full of imperfections because their goal is only to reach hereafter seeking the pleasure of Allah. They recognize that true happiness and peace will only be found in what is with Allah. This is the real true love that strengthens as opposed to infatuation and love that weakens a soul.

The Blissful Union ©2017 Syed ISBN 978-93-5268-923-1

Piece of Advice to my young brothers and sisters...

We see many a times in our families and societies today that many young brothers and sisters equally fall into this trap, where someone who is attracted to them, try to allure them into committing *Haram* (impermissible) acts with them. They have the intention to play with their emotions for a period of time, as long as their attraction lasts, and then throw them away to play this game with someone else. We advice our brothers and sisters to fear Allah and think for a moment ,would you want someone to do this with your close ones? Would you want that someone deceives and fools you in the same manner? Would you like someone to cheat you and disgrace you with similar acts? Give it a thought O young people! And remember that what goes around comes around.

Choosing your soulmate

Before we start talking about choosing one's spouse, we would like to mention that it is the right of the one seeking to get married that they have full freedom to choose who they want to get married to, within the limits of the *Sharee'ah* (Islamic legislation).
Islam teaches us very beautiful lessons in what we should look for while choosing our life partner.

Messenger of Allah (ﷺ) said in a hadith reported by Imam Al-Bukhari in his *Saheeh* no. 5090

" تُنْكَحُ الْمَرْأَةُ لأَرْبَعٍ لِمَالِهَا وَلِحَسَبِهَا وَجَمَالِهَا وَلِدِينِهَا، فَاظْفَرْ بِذَاتِ الدِّينِ تَرِبَتْ يَدَاكَ "

"A woman may be married for four things: her wealth, her lineage, her beauty and her religious commitment. Seek the one who is religiously-committed, may your hands be rubbed with dust (i.e., may you prosper)"

Shaykh Ibn Uthaymeen explained this *hadith* in *Sharh Riyadh as-Saliheen* (3/244): And its meaning is that the people in their customs seek in women these four characteristics. So its upon you to hold firmly and choose person of religious commitment and prosper.

Imam Nawawi said in explanation of above *hadith* in *Sharh Muslim* (10/51-52):
The correct meaning of this *hadith* is that the Prophet (peace and blessings of Allah be upon him) talks about what is done by the people in their customs, for they seek these four characteristics, the last of which in their view is religious commitment, but you who are seeking to follow the right way

should seek the one who is religiously committed. This is not a command to do so… This *hadith* encourages us to seek the company of religiously-committed people in all things, because the one who keeps company with them benefits from their good attitude and good ways, and will be safe from any bad influence from them.

Imam Abdurrahman Mubarakpuri said in *Tuhfat al-Ahwadhi Sharh Tirmidhi* (4/174) in explanation of above *hadith*: Al-Qaadi said: It is from the practice of the people to aspire in women and choose her for one of these qualities. It befits those who are religiously-devoted to base their actions on religious guidance, especially with regard to matters that are serious and have lasting effects.

What we can relate to from this *hadith* is, in today's time and age, when people seek for a spouse the first things that they look for are usually someone who is wealthy or beautiful or someone who carries a good family name. They stress and give a lot of importance to the worldly matters and some go so far that they are even ready to compromise on their religion and character.

In this *hadith*, our beloved messenger (ﷺ), teaches us that even though it is permissible for one to look for other characteristics, the one who chooses religion above all these things will truly succeed and prosper.

Here is an interesting parable in explanation of the above *hadith*. Al Hafidh al Mizzi states in *Tahdheeb al-Kamaal* (11/194):

"Yahya bin Yayha an Neesaboori said: I was with Sufyan ibn Uyaynah when a man approached him and said: "O Abu Muhammad, I came to complain to you about my wife, I am the most lowly and disliked of things to her."

Sufyan remained silent for a while then said: “It may be that you were only interested in her to increase yourself in honor.” The man said: “Yes, O Abu Muhammad.”

Sufyan said: “Whoever seeks honor [by marrying a woman] will be tested with lowliness, and whoever seeks wealth [by marrying a woman] will be tested with poverty, but whoever looks for righteousness [in a woman], then Allah would combine both honor and wealth with righteousness for him in her.” He then told him a story, he said:

“We were four brothers; Muhammad, ‘Imran, Ibraheem and me. Muhammad was the oldest, ‘Imran was the youngest and I was in between.When Muhammad wanted to get married, he was interested in lineage, so he married a woman of better lineage than him, so Allah tested him with lowliness.

Imran was interested in wealth, so he married a woman who was wealthier than him, so Allah tested him with poverty. They took his wealth and didn’t give him anything.

So I pondered over their affair. Ma’mar ibn Rashid traveled to us so I spoke to him about the affair and told him of their story. He reminded me of the a*hadith* that Aisha and Yahya ibn Ja’dah narrated. As for Ja’dah’s Hadith; the Prophet (ﷺ),- said: “A woman is married for four reasons: righteousness, lineage, wealth and beauty. Marry the one with righteousness and you will be successful.”

Aisha’s *hadith* is as follows; the Prophet (ﷺ) said: “The woman with the greatest blessing is the one with the least *Mahr*” So I chose righteousness and a small dowry, following the Sunnah of the Messenger (ﷺ), so Allah combined honor, wealth and righteousness for me [in my wife]”. [8]

---

[8] Taken from translation of Abu Abdul-Waahid Nadir Ahmad

Unrealistic expectations

Many young people today have unrealistic expectations of what they want in their spouse. These expectations many a times blind them and become barriers in their marriage. They miss out much better opportunities and people. Some sisters dream of their spouse to be rich like Abdurrahman bin Awf, with the generosity of Abu Bakr, the *Imaan* of Bilal, bravery of Khalid bin Waleed ...some sisters might say that they want their husband to have even half the beauty of Prophet Yusuf and be wise, caring, loving and funny at the same time. They think that their husband will come as a customized all-in-one package and they will live happily ever after.

While some of our brothers want a *Hoor* walking out of *Jannah* who they meet while walking on the street and it suddenly happens to be love at first sight. They even want her to be a pro at cooking, having expertise in house management and who knows the rights of her husband.

Five years down the line, when they don't find anyone to their liking, they realize they want to settle with someone who is a good practicing muslim. If only they realized it earlier!

Know that, true success lies in prioritizing the religious commitment and following the prophetic guidance. The most beautiful person is the one who is religious, and who has good character. This is the only beauty that will last forever. Every other materialistic matter will fade away with time.

This does not mean that we don't give importance to other issues like looks but what is meant is that the religious commitment should be given priority over all other things.

A brother was helping young people find good matches. He would ask them to email him the list of things they want in their spouse so he could see if there was anyone suitable for them. A girl emailed him stating what she was looking for and

The Blissful Union ©2017 Syed ISBN 978-93-5268-923-1

this was her description: "I want my husband to be as handsome as Brad Pitt while having the *taqwa* of Umar bin Al Khattab." The brother apologized saying he found no such person on the list.

Remember that a perfect marriage is not between two perfect people but between two imperfect people who learn when to overlook their imperfections.

The Blissful Union ©2017 Syed ISBN 978-93-5268-923-1

The recommendation of presenting one's daughter to a man of religion

Allah has mentioned in Al-Quran (28:23-28):

وَلَمَّا وَرَدَ مَآءَ مَدۡيَنَ وَجَدَ عَلَيۡهِ أُمَّةٗ مِّنَ ٱلنَّاسِ يَسۡقُونَ وَوَجَدَ مِن دُونِهِمُ ٱمۡرَأَتَيۡنِ
تَذُودَانِۖ قَالَ مَا خَطۡبُكُمَاۖ قَالَتَا لَا نَسۡقِي حَتَّىٰ يُصۡدِرَ ٱلرِّعَآءُۖ وَأَبُونَا شَيۡخٞ كَبِيرٞ
(٢٣) فَسَقَىٰ لَهُمَا ثُمَّ تَوَلَّىٰٓ إِلَى ٱلظِّلِّ فَقَالَ رَبِّ إِنِّي لِمَآ أَنزَلۡتَ إِلَيَّ مِنۡ خَيۡرٖ فَقِيرٞ
(٢٤) فَجَآءَتۡهُ إِحۡدَىٰهُمَا تَمۡشِي عَلَى ٱسۡتِحۡيَآءٖ قَالَتۡ إِنَّ أَبِي يَدۡعُوكَ لِيَجۡزِيَكَ أَجۡرَ
مَا سَقَيۡتَ لَنَاۚ فَلَمَّا جَآءَهُۥ وَقَصَّ عَلَيۡهِ ٱلۡقَصَصَ قَالَ لَا تَخَفۡۖ نَجَوۡتَ مِنَ ٱلۡقَوۡمِ
ٱلظَّٰلِمِينَ (٢٥) قَالَتۡ إِحۡدَىٰهُمَا يَٰٓأَبَتِ ٱسۡتَـٔۡجِرۡهُۖ إِنَّ خَيۡرَ مَنِ ٱسۡتَـٔۡجَرۡتَ ٱلۡقَوِيُّ
ٱلۡأَمِينُ (٢٦) قَالَ إِنِّيٓ أُرِيدُ أَنۡ أُنكِحَكَ إِحۡدَى ٱبۡنَتَيَّ هَٰتَيۡنِ عَلَىٰٓ أَن تَأۡجُرَنِي
ثَمَٰنِيَ حِجَجٖۖ فَإِنۡ أَتۡمَمۡتَ عَشۡرٗا فَمِنۡ عِندِكَۖ وَمَآ أُرِيدُ أَنۡ أَشُقَّ عَلَيۡكَۚ سَتَجِدُنِيٓ
إِن شَآءَ ٱللَّهُ مِنَ ٱلصَّٰلِحِينَ (٢٧) قَالَ ذَٰلِكَ بَيۡنِي وَبَيۡنَكَۖ أَيَّمَا ٱلۡأَجَلَيۡنِ قَضَيۡتُ فَلَا
عُدۡوَٰنَ عَلَيَّۖ وَٱللَّهُ عَلَىٰ مَا نَقُولُ وَكِيلٞ (٢٨

And when he arrived at the water of *Madyan* (Midian) he found there a group of men watering (their flocks), and besides them he found two women who were keeping back (their flocks). He said: "What is the matter with you?" They said: "We cannot water (our flocks) until the shepherds take (their flocks). And our father is a very old man." (23) So he watered (their flocks) for them, then he turned back to shade, and said: "My Lord! truly, I am in need of whatever good that You bestow on me!" (24) Then there came to him one of the two women, walking shyly. She said: "Verily, my father calls you that he may reward you for having watered (our flocks) for us." So when he came to him and narrated the story, he said: "Fear you not. You have escaped from the people who are *Zalimun* (polytheists, disbelievers, and wrong-doers)." (25) And said one of them (the two women): "O my father! Hire him! Verily, the best of men for you to hire is the strong, the trustworthy." (26)

He said: "I intend to wed one of these two daughters of mine to you, on condition that you serve me for eight years, but if you complete ten years, it will be (a favor) from you. But I intend not to place you under a difficulty. If Allah wills, you will find me one of the righteous." (27) He [Musa (Moses)] said: "That (is settled) between me and you whichever of the two terms I fulfill, there will be no injustice to me, and Allah is Surety over what we say." (28)

From this *ayah*, we come to know that the old man who was father of those girls, presented one of his daughter in marriage to a righteous person, a Prophet of Allah.

Imam al-Qurtubi said in his *Tafseer* (13/271) in explanation of this ayah:

فَمِنَ الْحَسَنِ عَرْضُ الرَّجُلِ وَلِيَّتَهُ، وَالْمَرْأَةُ نَفْسَهَا عَلَى الرَّجُلِ الصَّالِحِ

"So it is from the excellence that a man presents his daughter or the woman presents herself to a righteous man."

There is an astonishing story of a great scholar from *Tabi'een*, Imam Sa'eed bin Musayyib *rahimahullah*, in this regard. Who is Sa'eed bin Musayyib? He is called "The Leader of the *Tabi'een*", he studied and narrated from Uthman bin Affan, Ali bin Abi Talib, Sa'd bin Abi Waqqas, Hakeem bin Hizaam, Abdullah bin Abbas, Abdullah bin Umar, Abdullah bin 'Amr Bin Al-'Aas and so many other companions. May Allah be pleased with them all.

Imam Abu Nuaym narrated in his *Hilya al-Awliyaa* (2/167) with an authentic chain of narrators and also by Imam ad-Dhahabi in his *Siyar A'lam an-Nubalaa* (4/233):

The Blissful Union ©2017 Syed ISBN 978-93-5268-923-1

"Abdullah bin Abu Wada'a related: I used to keep the company of Sa'eed bin Musayyib. He missed me for several days and enquired about me from people. When I came back, he said, "Where have you been?" I said, I was busy because my wife had died. Sa'eed said, "Why didn't you tell me? Even I would have attended the funeral." Then when I wanted to leave, he said: "Would not you remarry?" I said, May Allah have mercy on you, who could do that. I have only two or three dirhams. He said, "I will give you my daughter in marriage." I asked: Will you? He said: "Yes."
Then he started to praise Allah Almighty and ask Allah to have peace and blessings upon the Prophet. Then, he married me to his daughter with two-dirhams (or three) as a dowry. I was very happy. I went home and started to think of someone to lend me money. I was fasting on that day. After I performed the *maghrib* prayer I went home to break my fast which was only bread and olive oil. I heard someone knocking the door. I said, Who is that? He said, "Sa'eed." I started thinking about different people with the name Sa'eed. I could not even think of Sa'eed bin Musayyib because for forty years I didn't see him going anywhere from his house except Masjid. I did not expect his coming.

I thought that he changed his mind. I said, O Abu Muhammad! Would you inform, I would have come to you. He said, "You are worthy to be visited." I asked: What do you want me to do? He said, "You were a single man and you have already married. I dislike that you spend that night alone. This is your wife." She was standing behind him at that time. Then he gave her to me and left. Indeed she was a very beautiful and knowledgeable woman who had memorized Quran and *ahadith* of Messenger of Allah (ﷺ) and she knew how to fulfill the rights of a husband.

The Blissful Union ©2017 Syed ISBN 978-93-5268-923-1

It is worth mentioning that Imam Sa'eed bin Musayyib had refused to give his daughter in marriage to the son of the caliph of Muslims, Abdul-Malik bin Marwan.

Imam Abu Dawood reported in his *Kitaab az-Zuhd* no.425 with an authentic chain of narration, that Imam Sa'eed bin Musayyib refused to give his daughter in marriage to Prince Waleed bin Abdul Malik, who was son of caliph of muslims, Abdul-Malik bin Marwan.

Subhanallah!! What an example! This great *Tab'iee* Imam Saeed bin Musayyib refused proposal of a Prince and gave his daughter to a poor man whose wife had died. Why? It's because he gave precedence to religion over everything.

The Blissful Union ©2017 Syed ISBN 978-93-5268-923-1

Marrying a person of innovation

Allah says in Al-Quran (4:140):

وَقَدْ نَزَّلَ عَلَيْكُمْ فِى ٱلْكِتَٰبِ أَنْ إِذَا سَمِعْتُمْ ءَايَٰتِ ٱللَّهِ يُكْفَرُ بِهَا وَيُسْتَهْزَأُ بِهَا فَلَا تَقْعُدُوا۟ مَعَهُمْ حَتَّىٰ يَخُوضُوا۟ فِى حَدِيثٍ غَيْرِهِۦٓ ۚ إِنَّكُمْ إِذًا مِّثْلُهُمْ ۗ إِنَّ ٱللَّهَ جَامِعُ ٱلْمُنَٰفِقِينَ وَٱلْكَٰفِرِينَ فِى جَهَنَّمَ جَمِيعًا

"And it has already been revealed to you in the Book (this Qur'an) that when you hear the Verses of Allah being denied and mocked at, then sit not with them, until they engage in a talk other than that; (but if you stayed with them) certainly in that case you would be like them. Surely, Allah will collect the hypocrites and disbelievers all together in Hell."

Imam Qurtubi said in *tafseer* of this ayah in *Tafseer* Qurtubi (7/142): A group from people of *Sunnah* agreed that this *ayah* refers to everyone who sits with people of innovation and maintains any kind of relationship with them.

There is a *hadith* reported by Imam Al-Ajury in his book *Ash-Sharee'ah* no. 2040, with an authentic chain that Messenger of Allah (ﷺ) said:

من وقّر صَاحِبُ بِدْعَة فَقَد أَعَانَ عَلَى هَدَم الإسْلاَم

"Whoever honors an innovator has aided in destruction of Islam."

If it is prohibited to sit with people of innovation, to honour them and to have relationship with them, then how about the one who chooses to live their life with them? And what about the offspring that will come from this marriage?

Imam Ibn Asaakir reported a story of Imran bin Hattan in his *Tareekh Dimashq* (43/489):

Imran bin Hattan married a woman from *Khawarij* in order to change her from the path of *khawarij* but she converted him to path of *khawarij*. She was the most beautiful woman amongst people with a good intellect.
Finally he ended up becoming one of the leaders of the *Khawarij*. Allah's refuge is sought.

Shaykh Ahmad bin Yahya an-Najmee explained the following statement of Imam Fudayl bin Iyaad: "Whoever marries his beloved daughter to an innovator has cut off the ties of relationship with her."

Shaykh explained it in his *Irshad as-Saree ila Sharh as-Sunnah lil Barbaharee* (*Explanation of the Creed of Al-Barbahaaree*[9]) (no.137): "In this statement is a prohibition of marring your beloved daughter to an innovator and being loose towards them, all of that is prohibited, and it is a stern warning about mixing with and befriending innovators as we have mentioned before."

---

9 published by (Maktabah Daar al-Manhaaj)

Giving your Daughter in Marriage to one who does not pray

A question was asked to Shaykh Abdul Azeez Bin Baaz as recorded in *Fatawa Islamiyyah, Darussalam*, volume 5, pages 173/174

Q: "One of my kin has proposed to my daughter and I am under an obligation to him, (for example, for having lent him money, or shown some kindness to him etc.) but he is addicted to alcohol and he keeps company with bad people and prays little, or does not pray at all. He is also addicted to watching videos and television and other time-wasting devices and I am in difficulty regarding him. I request clarification of the ruling of Islam in the matter."

Answer:
"If the person proposing to your daughter is as you have described him, then it is not permissible for you to give her in marriage to him, because she is a trust in your hands, so it is incumbent for you to choose for her the most righteous man in his religion and his character."
It is not permissible for a person who does not pray to be married to a Muslim woman who does pray, since he is not a suitable match for her, because abandoning the prayer is an act of major disbelief, according to the saying of the Prophet (ﷺ): "Between a man and polytheism and disbelief is the abandonment of prayer." (Muslim no.82)

And the saying of the Prophet (ﷺ):

"The covenant between us and them is prayer; whoever abandons it has committed an act of disbelief." (*At-Tirmidhi no. 2621)*

Narrated by Imam Ahmad and the compilers of the *Sunan*, with an authentic chain of narrators.

There are many other evidences in the Book (of Allah) and the Sunnah which prove the disbelief of one who abandons the prayer, even if he does not reject its obligation, according to the most correct of two opinions held by the scholars. However, if he rejects its obligation or mocked it, then he is guilty of major disbelief according to the consensus of the Muslims.

As for the one who drinks alcohol but prays, he is not guilty of disbelief by doing this, as long as he does not claim that it is permissible, but he has committed a major sin and he has gone astray thereby. Therefore, it is lawful for you not to give her in marriage to him, even if he prays, due to his sin and because he might lead his wife and children to this great crime.

We ask Allah to improve the situation of the Muslims and guide them to His Straight Path, and to preserve us and them from obeying vain desires and Satan, for verily, He is Most Generous, Most Noble.

The Blissful Union ©2017 Syed ISBN 978-93-5268-923-1

Few points of advice for finding the right spouse

1) Make *Dua*

Dua is the most powerful thing a believer could use. If you were to ask your mother for something and she didn't give it to you, then you kept nagging and begging her for it and after a few tears roll down your eyes, wouldn't she give it to you? A mother is the one who has a very soft corner in her heart for her children. But do you know how Allah is?

Prophet (ﷺ) mentioned in a *hadith* narrated by Imam Al-Bukhari in his *Saheeh* no.5999 that, Allah is more merciful to His servant than his mother is to him. Just like a mother wouldn't want to throw her child into the fire, Allah is much more merciful to His slaves.

So imagine if you were to beg Allah for something, crying your heart out to Him, you think He wouldn't grant you what you ask for? Sometimes we get deceived thinking our invocations do not get answered, but know that if He doesn't give you exactly what you asked for, He will definitely always give you something much better than that; something that will save you from destruction in this life and hereafter. All we have to have is faith and never give up on asking Him even if it were to ask Him for something very small like a bite of food or a sip of water. Remember that Allah is The Only One who controls the entire universe and in His Hand is the entire dominion. Our beloved Prophet (ﷺ) when giving advice to the young lad Abdullah bin Abbas:

إذا سألت فاسأل الله...

"If you ask, then ask Allah..."

If nothing else then think about Musa عليه السلام when he was running away from Pharaoh to the city of *Madyan* after he mistakenly killed a man. What did he do when he reached *Madyan* and was sitting under the shade? He made *Dua* to Allah saying:

ربِّ انّي لِما أنزلت إليَّ من خير فقير

"O my Lord. I am in dire need of any good that you send down upon me."

After he made this *dua*, Allah immediately blessed him with a choice to marry one of the two sisters. So, do not ever underestimate the power of invoking Allah.

2) Seek help from those who are righteous and wise

Do not use Facebook, Instagram, QQ, Q-Zone, WeChat, Whats app or Twitter to find your spouse. There are high possibilities that you will find an ignorant who was pretending to be a student of knowledge to get more likes and shares. In real life, when you spend a day with him, you will find that he does not pray or that he is a smoker . Maybe a small percentage of marriages fixed through Facebook or Instagram, successfully work out but the harms of going through social media outweighs the benefits. So be careful! Not everyone who shows they are religious or scholarly turn out to be so.

What you can do though is to ask someone in your circle of family or friends, whom you can trust and who are known for their piety, to help you find someone. There are higher chances of finding the right person if you ask someone who knows both you and the person they are going to recommend for you. Also, accompanying the people who are known for their righteousness will open up your chances of finding a righteous spouse.

3) Let your parents know

Many young people shy away from letting their parents know about their want to get married. They become afraid that their parents might react strangely to them. There are parents who do react strangely after hearing such a thing from their children. If you are not very close to your parents, you can either ask one of your siblings or your other family members who you are close to, to help you out. Try sending your parents a message or an email. Do this in a manner you are comfortable with. Since they are your parents, there is a high chance they will understand you.

4) Attend Islamic classes

We should not expect to find a religiously committed sister or a brother at the birthday-anniversary parties or a *Niqab* wearing (veiled) sister and bearded brother at the free-mixing social clubs. It will not be of any help sitting at home, thinking yourself about, why you are still single. Be at good places like attending a Islamic classes at the Masjid or an Islamic centre based on Quran and Sunnah upon the understanding of the companions. This will open up the doors for you to meet the right people. Once you get to know them,, you can send the proposal to her *Wali*.

5) Educate yourself about marriage

First, how do you describe yourself?

"I'm completely amazing and awesome. The person that will marry me will definitely be very luck. "If your answer to the above question is anywhere near it, then know that you are definitely not ready for marriage. Just because you have reached the age of twenty and are physically ready for marriage doesn't make you truly ready for it. Marriage is much more than intimacy. It requires adjustment and compromise between both spouses. It is a relationship where both spouses walk together in the ups and downs of life, being supportive of each other. This requires a lot of maturity and understanding because marriage, even though a very beautiful bond, is not a bed full of roses.

What you have to also know that instead of completely concentrating on your partner's qualities all the time, you have to prepare yourself first and bring about the right changes. in you. What is your relationship with Allah? How will you be as a spouse? Do you know your rights and responsibilities? How should you fulfill the rights of your spouse? All too often people concentrate on finding the right spouse, realizing little that half of any marriage is being the right spouse. We get blinded by looking for the perfect spouse that we neglect ourselves. But if we were to sincerely work on ourselves and strive to become better individuals who are more caring and loving, showing respect to others, then things would work out more smoothly by the will of Allah. So try to learn about what Islam teaches about marriage, about what is mentioned in the Quran and what is taught in the Sunnah of the messenger (ﷺ).

Marriage by force

Islam gives both men and women full right to get married to the person of their choice. So the parents should fear Allah regarding this matter. They should not give their children in marriage except to someone their daughters and sons are pleased with, and those that are compatible and suitable for them. The guardian should not give his children in marriage for his own personal interests.

Imam Al-Bukhari narrates in his *Saheeh* under the chapter "The father or the guardian cannot give a virgin or matron in marriage without her consent", no. 5136:

لاَ تُنْكَحُ الأَيِّمُ حَتَّى تُسْتَأْمَرَ وَلاَ تُنْكَحُ الْبِكْرُ حَتَّى تُسْتَأْذَنَ ". قَالُوا يَا رَسُولَ اللَّهِ
وَكَيْفَ إِذْنُهَا قَالَ " أَنْ تَسْكُتَ

"The Prophet (ﷺ) said, "A matron should not be given in marriage except after consulting her; and a virgin should not be given in marriage except after her permission." The people asked, "O Allah's Messenger (ﷺ)! How can we know her permission?" He said, Her silence (indicates her permission)"

Many parents even try to manipulate their children to get married to someone against their choice. The parents do it for various reasons. Parents may have made a promise when the child was young and they feel they can't let the other family down. They want their children to get married to a person who is wealthy or of a high family status even if their daughter and son hate the idea of being with that person. Many brothers and sisters are subject to emotional blackmail and physical threats. A number of them may be forced to marry a member of their extended family, for example, a cousin.

Sometimes, their relatives are emotionally blackmailing them by threatening to cut off family ties.

What parents often do not realize is that in wanting to keep their relatives and other people happy, they destroy the lives of their own children. This has adverse effects on individuals, families and societies. It disturbs the lives of both partners even if one partner is unhappy with the marriage because they will be unable to fulfill the rights of their spouse. What is the use of such a marriage where there is no love and compassion whereas the purpose of marriage in Islam is that the married couple finds tranquility and peace through love and mercy between them? Most of the forced marriages end up either in divorce or in both spouses being psychologically disturbed. Those who compromise by living together, the children that are born out of this marriage will also live unstable lives seeing their parents unhappy with one another.

The ruling on such marriages in Islam is that they are invalid. Imam Al-Bukhari narrates in his *Saheeh* under the chapter "If a man gives his daughter in marriage while she is averse to it, then such marriage is invalid", no. 5138:

عَنْ خَنْسَاءَ بِنْتِ خِذَامٍ الأَنْصَارِيَّةِ، أَنَّ أَبَاهَا، زَوَّجَهَا وَهْىَ ثَيِّبٌ، فَكَرِهَتْ ذَلِكَ
فَأَتَتْ رَسُولَ اللَّهِ صلى الله عليه وسلم فَرَدَّ نِكَاحَهُ.

"Khansa bint Khidam Al-Ansariya narrated that her father gave her in marriage when she was a matron and she disliked that marriage. So she went to Allah's Messenger (ﷺ) and he declared that marriage invalid."

Imam Ibn Majah narrated in his *Sunan* no.1874 with an authentic chain of narration:

جَاءَتْ فَتَاةٌ إِلَى النَّبِيِّ ـ صلى الله عليه وسلم ـ فَقَالَتْ إِنَّ أَبِي زَوَّجَنِي ابْنَ أَخِيهِ لِيَرْفَعَ بِي خَسِيسَتَهُ . قَالَ فَجَعَلَ الأَمْرَ إِلَيْهَا . فَقَالَتْ قَدْ أَجَزْتُ مَا صَنَعَ أَبِي وَلَكِنْ أَرَدْتُ أَنْ تَعْلَمَ النِّسَاءُ أَنْ لَيْسَ إِلَى الآبَاءِ مِنَ الأَمْرِ شَىْءٌ

“A girl came to the Prophet and said: 'My father married me to his brother's son so that he might raise his status thereby.' The Prophet gave her the choice, and she said, I approve of what my father did, but I wanted women to know that their fathers have no right to do that.”

Forced marriages and their effects are experienced in all communities and you will find it in every place and time regardless of a person’s religion, race or culture.

A girl was well educated and brought up in a religiously practicing society. Her father wanted her to get married to a man from within their community. Her uncle suggested someone for her and her father agreed to it. But the girl was unwilling to get married to this boy because he came from a very different background and was brought up in very different environment. The girl knew that her ideology wouldn't match his, and that she wouldn’t be able to adjust to his way of life. But her father was persistent in his decision and he involved other family members to convince her for the marriage. The girl cried and pleaded that she didn't want to get married to this man but they all forced her to say yes for him. Finally they got her married to this man. The girl found it very difficult to adjust herself because her perspective of a spouse was completely different from this man. She tried very hard to adapt but she was failed. There was no compatibility between them. They couldn't even hold a proper conversation, not even for a few minutes straight. She wasn't even able to be intimate with him because her heart just didn't love him even though she would allow him to be intimate with her.

The husband's mother mistreated the girl and called her names. One year passed and the problems between the two only increased. The girl went back to her father's house. Her relatives tried to reconcile between them but it was of no use. As a final resort, they got the boy to sit down to talk to the girl. She got ready for it, but the boy reacted disrespectfully with the girl and her father. He started cursing them and left the lace stating that he would divorce the girl. As their divorce took place, the girl was completely shattered. She couldn't imagine that this is how the most important decision of her life, the most significant part of her life, would end. She lost all her hopes and fell into depression but kept invoking Allah to get her out of this difficulty. Even her father became distressed. She had no bad feelings towards her previous husband and had forgiven him for what he had done towards the end. Allah answered her supplication and again blessed her with second marriage. But this time to a man whom she liked, someone compatible and suitable for her. Someone who was brought up in the same place and environment as hers. They both knew that they would be able to live their lives together. All praise is due to Allah that they are now happily married.

A girl was known for her beauty in her town. Her parents chose a boy for her only because he very wealthy. He was neither good looking nor did he have an impressive personality. The girl didn't like him whatsoever, yet her parents forced her to marry him. She was extremely unhappy with this marriage and she became completely depressed. For a very long time, there was no intimacy in their marriage. She wanted to get rid of him somehow and wanted divorce, but her parents were unwilling to let her do so. She tried a lot but to no avail. Then she thought of accusing him of being impotent.

The Blissful Union ©2017 Syed ISBN 978-93-5268-923-1

That's when members from both families sat down together to try to reconcile the matter. The boy told them that he was not impotent, rather she didn't let him touch her even once. They forced her to go back with this man and live her life. She forcefully agreed and went back to live with him. She had to forcibly be intimate with him as well. She is still married to him and has children with him. She made up her mind to live life this way. She lost all her charm and beauty because of depression. In the eyes of people, she might be a happily married woman with children, but only she knows the pain and struggle she has been living with.

Shaykhul Islam Ibn Taymiyyah said in *Majmoo' al-Fataawa* (32/25):

وأمّا تزويجها مع كراهتها للنكاح ، فهذا مخالف للأصول والعقول ، والله لم يُسوِّغ لوليها أن يُكرهها على بيع أو إجارة إلا بإذنها ، ولا على طعام ، أو شراب ، أو لباس ، لا تريده ، فكيف يكرهها على مباضعة ومعاشرة من تكره مباضعته ! ، ومعاشرة من تكره معاشرته !.

والله قد جعل بن الزوجين مودةً ورحمة ، فإذا كان لا يحصل إلا مع بغضها له ونفورها عنه ، فأيُّ مودةٍ ورحمةٍ في ذلك !!

"As for giving her in marriage when she is unwilling, this is contrary to the basic principles and common sense. Moreover Allah did not allow her guardian to force her into buying or renting except with her permission, or to eat or drink or wear something that she does not want, so how can he force her into sleeping with and living with someone she hates to sleep with, and living with someone she does not want to live with.

Allah wants love and compassion between the spouses, and if that cannot be attained because of her dislike for him and her disinclination towards him, then what kind of love and compassion can there be in that case?!"

Istikhara Prayer

With regard to the *Istikhara* prayer, people around the world keep various wrong beliefs and misconceptions. A myth that is widespread among people is that after praying *istikhara,* one should sleep, and whatever good one sees in their dream that makes him happy means that what they want to do is good and will be made easy for him, otherwise it is not good. Many people perform this prayer several times for a matter they are confused about, and others believe that if they pray *istikhara* when they are confused, Allah will send them a sign to choose the correct option. Still many others believe that they will see in their dream things like a shoe with a sweet inside or some other sign of good or bad omen. Some people also say that "if the decision I am going to take is good for me, I'll see something pleasant or something green in colour in my dream, and if decision is not good for me, I ll see bad dream or something black or red." None of the above mentioned beliefs and concepts about *Istikhara* is correct as they are not found in the Quran or authentic sunnah. The correct position is that when Allah makes something easy for you, after having decreed it and accepted your *dua* , this is a sign that it is good to go ahead and do it. The existence of obstacles and difficulties is an indication that Allah is pushing His slave away from doing it.

The correct way to perform the *istikhara* is mentioned below.

Firstly, before performing *Istikhara* prayer, you should think about and consider all the options for which you are seeking guidance from Allah. Allah has blessed every human being with an intellect and ability to think. In the case of choosing your spouse, use your intellect, research about him/her, find

The Blissful Union ©2017 Syed ISBN 978-93-5268-923-1

out about their religious commitment through various means and contemplate on it.

Secondly, you should seek counsel and advice from the wise and knowledgeable people in your community. You should seek advice from the people who are sincere, honest and the one who cares about you, people who are experienced and mature, and who have close connection with their Creator, so that they have a well-rounded perspective which they can provide you.

And finally, once you have made a final decision about the matter at hand, for example once you decide that you are going to marry someone (not when you are confused), you should pray two *rakah* of voluntary prayer and recite this *dua* after prayer.

اللَّهُمَّ إِنِّي أَسْتَخِيرُكَ بِعِلْمِكَ وَأَسْتَقْدِرُكَ بِقُدْرَتِكَ وَأَسْأَلُكَ مِنْ فَضْلِكَ الْعَظِيمِ فَإِنَّكَ
تَقْدِرُ وَلَا أَقْدِرُ وَتَعْلَمُ وَلَا أَعْلَمُ وَأَنْتَ عَلَّامُ الْغُيُوبِ اللَّهُمَّ إِنْ كُنْتَ تَعْلَمُ أَنَّ هَذَا
الْأَمْرَ خَيْرٌ لِي فِي دِينِي وَمَعَاشِي وَعَاقِبَةِ أَمْرِي فَاقْدُرْهُ لِي وَيَسِّرْهُ لِي ثُمَّ بَارِكْ
لِي فِيهِ وَإِنْ كُنْتَ تَعْلَمُ أَنَّ هَذَا الْأَمْرَ شَرٌّ فِي دِينِي وَمَعَاشِي وَعَاقِبَةِ أَمْرِي
فَاصْرِفْهُ عَنِّي وَاصْرِفْنِي عَنْهُ وَاقْدُرْ لِيَ الْخَيْرَ حَيْثُ كَانَ ثُمَّ ارْضِنِي بِهِ

Allaahumma inni astakheeruka bi 'ilmika wa astaqdiruka bi qudratika wa as'aluka min fadlika, fa innaka taqdiru wa laa aqdir, wa ta'lamu wa laa a'lam, wa anta 'allaam al-ghuyoob. Allaahumma fa in kunta ta'lamu haadha'l-amra (then the matter should be mentioned by name) khayran li fi 'aajil amri wa aajilihi (or: fi deeni wa ma'aashi wa 'aaqibati amri) faqdurhu li wa yassirhu li thumma baarik li fihi. Allaahumma wa in kunta ta'lamu annahu sharrun li fi deeni wa ma'aashi wa 'aaqibati amri (or: fi 'aajili amri wa aajilihi) fasrifni 'anhu [wasrafhu 'anni] waqdur li al-khayr haythu kaana thumma radini bihi

"O Allah! I ask guidance from Your knowledge, And Power from Your Might and I ask for Your great blessings. You are capable and I am not. You know and I do not and You know the unseen. O Allah! If You know that this thing is good for my religion and my subsistence and in my Hereafter (or if it is better for my present and later needs), then You ordain it for me and make it easy for me to get, And then bless me in it, and if You know that this thing is harmful to me In my religion and subsistence and in the Hereafter (or if it is worse for my present and later needs), then keep it away from me and let me be away from it. And ordain for me whatever is good for me, And make me satisfied with it". The Prophet added that then the person should name (mention) his need.

This *dua* is reported in an authentic *hadith* by Imam Al-Bukhari in his *Saheeh* no.1166.

Reviver of the Twentieth Century Shaykh Al-Albani was asked questions regarding *Istikhara* prayer, which are reproduced below.

Question: "What should the one making *istikhara* prayer say if he has two affairs on the same level and does not have an inclination toward either one, meaning 50-50?"

Shaykh al-Albani answers: "What I understand from your question is that he does not have an intention (to do something), therefore there is no *istikhara* prayer upon him."

Question: "Is the *istikhara* prayer legislated for one who is confused about doing something or is it legislated for one who has made up his mind to do so?"

Shaykh al-Albani answers: "No, the *istikhara* prayer does not remove confusion. *Istikhara* prayer is (done) after a person has made up his mind to do something; so here, *istikhara* is performed. *Istikhara* prayer is not legislated for removing doubt and uncertainty regarding a matter which the Muslim has not made up his mind about."

Question: "Is the duʿa (supplication) of *istikhara* prayer before the *taslim* or after it?"

Shaykh al-Albani answers: "After the *taslim.*"

Question: "Is it allowed to repeat the *istikhara* prayer?"

Shaykh al-Albani answers: "It is allowed if his *istikhara* prayer was not (performed in the way in which it is) legislated, and it is enough for it to be not legislated if he makes *istikhara* to his Lord by (merely) his words, and not by his heart. And he himself is aware of this inattentiveness, so then he is forced to repeat (the *istikhara* prayer). As for if he himself did not feel any of that, then he has innovated (if he repeats it)."[10]

---

[10] Source: Silsilat ul-huda wan-nur (the series of guidance and light) of Shaykh Al- Albani tape no. 206 (a), 664 (b), 426 (c) translated by asaheeha translations

The first glance: looking at the prospective spouse

Islam commands us to lower our gaze and not to look at the ones who are *haram* for us to look at; *the non mahrams*. However, it gives an exception and allows us to look at the one with whom you want to get married. This is to help you make your marriage decision as you are going to live the rest of your life with this person. There are many evidences from the Sunnah that says that looking at the prospective spouse is allowed.

It is reported in *Sunan an-Nasa'ee* no.3247 in an authentic narration:

عَنْ أَبِي هُرَيْرَةَ، أَنَّ رَجُلاً، أَرَادَ أَنْ يَتَزَوَّجَ، امْرَأَةً فَقَالَ النَّبِيُّ صلى الله عليه وسلم " انْظُرْ إِلَيْهَا فَإِنَّ فِي أَعْيُنِ الأَنْصَارِ شَيْئًا "

"It was narrated from Abu Hurairah that a man wanted to marry a woman and the Prophet said: 'Look at her, for there is something in the eyes of the Ansar.'"

It is also reported in *Sunan Ibn Majah* no.1938 with an authentic chain of narration:

عَنْ أَنَسِ بْنِ مَالِكٍ، أَنَّ الْمُغِيرَةَ بْنَ شُعْبَةَ، أَرَادَ أَنْ يَتَزَوَّجَ، امْرَأَةً فَقَالَ لَهُ النَّبِيُّ - صلى الله عليه وسلم - " اذْهَبْ فَانْظُرْ إِلَيْهَا فَإِنَّهُ أَحْرَى أَنْ يُؤْدَمَ بَيْنَكُمَا " . فَفَعَلَ فَتَزَوَّجَهَا فَذَكَرَ مِنْ مُوَافَقَتِهَا .

"It was narrated from Anas bin Malik that Mughirah bin Shubah wanted to marry a woman. The Prophet (ﷺ) said to him, 'Go and look at her, for that is more likely to create love between you.' So he did that, and married her, and mentioned how well he got along with her."

The Blissful Union ©2017 Syed ISBN 978-93-5268-923-1

And it is narrated in an authentic narration in *Sunan Abu Dawood* no.2082:

قَالَ رَسُولُ اللَّهِ صلى الله عليه وسلم " إِذَا خَطَبَ أَحَدُكُمُ الْمَرْأَةَ فَإِنِ اسْتَطَاعَ أَنْ يَنْظُرَ إِلَى مَا يَدْعُوهُ إِلَى نِكَاحِهَا فَلْيَفْعَلْ " . قَالَ فَخَطَبْتُ جَارِيَةً فَكُنْتُ أَتَخَبَّأُ لَهَا حَتَّى رَأَيْتُ مِنْهَا مَا دَعَانِي إِلَى نِكَاحِهَا وَتَزَوُّجِهَا فَتَزَوَّجْتُهَا

"The Prophet (ﷺ) said: When one of you ask a woman in marriage, if he is able to look at what will induce him to marry her, he should do so. He (Jabir) said, I asked a girl in marriage, I used to look at her secretly, until I looked at what induced me to marry her. I, therefore, married her."

There are many incidents, that we might think used to take place only in old times, but they even take place today where both the girl and boy who are going to get married have never seen each other before marriage. Their parents see the girl or the boy and they decide that their child will marry them. This causes great tribulations and sometimes such marriages come to the end even before they start, due to one or both of them not liking each other.

On the other extreme of this case is the people who take this issue so lightly that they not only look at the person they are going to get married to but they begin to behave the way married couples do with each other. They talk with each other for hours on the phone, chat through messages, and they meet each other secretly (i.e.,without any third person, or someone supervising their conversations). They indulge in all sorts of *Haram* (impermissible) acts. What is more surprising is that the parents have completely allowed their children and support them for such actions while everything takes place in front of their eyes. This creates great *fitnah* (trial) for both the girl and the boy because unlike marriage, engagement is not a contract but a mere exchange of words by both parties as a promise for marriage. So engagement does not make the two halal for each other, and it is not permissible for them to interact freely. And Allah is sought for aid.

The Blissful Union ©2017 Syed ISBN 978-93-5268-923-1

If a person has proposed marriage to a woman, it is not permissible for anyone else to offer a proposal to her

There is an authentic *hadith* reported in *Saheeh Al-Bukhari* no. 5142:

كَانَ يَقُولُ نَهَى النَّبِيُّ صلى الله عليه وسلم أَنْ يَبِيعَ بَعْضُكُمْ عَلَى بَيْعِ بَعْضٍ، وَلاَ يَخْطُبَ الرَّجُلُ عَلَى خِطْبَةِ أَخِيهِ، حَتَّى يَتْرُكَ الْخَاطِبُ قَبْلَهُ، أَوْ يَأْذَنَ لَهُ الْخَاطِبُ.

"Narrated Ibn Umar:The Prophet (ﷺ) decreed that one should not try to cancel a bargain already agreed upon between some other persons (by offering a bigger price). And a man should not ask for the hand of a girl who is already engaged to his Muslim brother, unless the first suitor gives her up, or allows him to ask for her hand."

Hafidh Ibn Hajr explained this *hadith* in *Fath ul Bari* (9/200), that if a girl has stated that she rejects the offer of the one who proposed her, then it is not prohibited for other person to send proposal. He also said that if the first suitor is immoral, a chaste man is permitted to propose over his proposal.
If such a situation occurs where a woman has accepted the proposal of a man and both of them have agreed to get married, and knowingly another man sends this engaged woman a proposal, this could cause great problems between individuals and the families involved, the problems such as severing of ties and breaking of brotherhood.

The engagement ceremony

Another tribulation that has afflicted the Muslims is having lavish and extravagant engagement parties.

Allah says in Al-Quran (7:31):

وَكُلُوا۟ وَٱشْرَبُوا۟ وَلَا تُسْرِفُوٓا۟ إِنَّهُۥ لَا يُحِبُّ ٱلْمُسْرِفِينَ

"And eat and drink but waste not by extravagance, certainly He (Allah) likes not *Al-Musrifun* (those who waste by extravagance)."

Some Muslim families arrange a big engagement ceremonies where all types of *Haraam* (impermissible) activities take place such as the free mixing between opposite genders and the playing of music. The engaging couples are made to sit on stage. Everyone including the *non mahram* can see them and the couples exchange their engagement rings. They put it on to the other's finger. While exchanging gifts or rings in itself is permissible, but some people attach impermissible beliefs to this act which makes the act of exchanging the gifts or rings impermissible.

Shaykh Ibn Uthaymeen rahimahullah said in *Al-Fataawa al-Jaami'ah li'l-Mar'ah al-Muslimah* (3/914) on the issue of engagement rings which they term as *Dublah*:

" '*Dublah*' is a word that refers to the engagement ring. The basic principle regarding it that there is nothing wrong with rings (i.e., they are permissible) , unless if they are accompanied by certain beliefs, as practiced by some people , that when the man writes his name on the ring that he gives to his fiancée, and the woman writes her name on the ring that she gives to her fiancé, they believe that this will guarantee the bonds between both of the spouses. In this case this *dublah* is *haram*, because it represents an attachment to something for which there is no basis in *sharee'ah* and which does not make sense. Similarly it is impermissible for the man to put the ring on the woman's hand himself, because she is not his wife yet, so she is still a stranger (i.e; *non-mahram*) for him; she is not his wife except after the marriage contract."

The Blissful Union ©2017 Syed ISBN 978-93-5268-923-1

The engagement period

Many people fail to realize, whether based on ignorance or while having knowledge, that the term 'engagement' only means a promise of marriage. This does not in any case make the two halal for each other. These individuals who have given each other a promise of marriage, take this as a freedom to talk to each other for hours on stretch through messages or phone calls. They even meet each other in public and private places. Doing these things are *Haram* (impermissible) by all means no matter how you present it. Engagements nowadays last for months and years for many reasons such as wanting to collect money for lavish weddings or they feel that both need time to get to know each other. Keeping engagements for long periods of time creates lot of *fitnah* (trials) and opens doors to many evils. There have been many cases where the engaged couples, believing that since they are going to get married to each other anyway, started meeting each other. They even had intimate relationships with each other. There have been cases where, after having grand celebrations of engagements and as the time passed, the engaged couples came to dislike each other and break their engagements. Islam does not allow all these things. Rather, as soon as a person decides to get married to the person of their choice, Islam prescribes *Nikah,* thus closing all the avenues that leads to *Haram* acts.

The Blissful Union ©2017 Syed ISBN 978-93-5268-923-1

Make marriage easy

When marriage becomes expensive, unlawful sexual encounters becomes cheap.
Today we are living in a society where marriage has become difficult and it is getting more and more difficult. Millions are spent to make this occasion of marriage grand. It does not make any sense to have expensive wedding ceremonies under the pretext of 'What will people say? or How will people react?

Our young generation today is falling for *Zina* (fornication) and other unlawful sexual encounters. They are unable to fulfill their desires in *halal* manner. They feel pressurized by our social custom of having extravagant weddings and dowries where they have to spend large sums of money. Our social custom makes it hard for the young people to afford to get married and to fulfill their desires in *halal* way.
The solution to this is to keep marriages as simple as possible , and stick to what Allah has prescribed in the matter of spending.

Allah says in Al-Quran (25:67):

وَٱلَّذِينَ إِذَآ أَنفَقُواْ لَمۡ يُسۡرِفُواْ وَلَمۡ يَقۡتُرُواْ وَكَانَ بَيۡنَ ذَٰلِكَ قَوَامٗا

"And those, who, when they spend, are neither extravagant nor niggardly, but hold a medium (way) between those (extremes)."

Allah also says about spending in Al-Quran (65:7):

لِيُنفِقْ ذُو سَعَةٍ مِّن سَعَتِهِۦ ۖ وَمَن قُدِرَ عَلَيْهِ رِزْقُهُۥ فَلْيُنفِقْ مِمَّآ ءَاتَىٰهُ ٱللَّهُ ۚ لَا يُكَلِّفُ ٱللَّهُ نَفْسًا إِلَّا مَآ ءَاتَىٰهَا ۚ سَيَجْعَلُ ٱللَّهُ بَعْدَ عُسْرٍ يُسْرًا

"Let the rich man spend according to his means, and the man whose resources are restricted, let him spend according to what Allah has given him. Allah puts no burden on any person beyond what He has given him. Allah will grant after hardship, ease."

The blessed marriage is not the one where huge sum of money is spent, rather the blessed marriage is the one where the spendings are the least and in which everything is made easy for the people.

It is reported by Imam Ibn Hibban in his *Saheeh* no.4034 with an authentic chain that the Prophet (ﷺ) said:

خير النكاح أيسره

"The blessed *Nikah* is the one that is the easiest"

Marriage is from the Sunnah

The dowry and Mahr

The practice of giving the dowry exists all over the world and it is as old as human civilization. But the way it is given differs from place to place. It is prevalent in most parts of the world like India, Pakistan, Bangladesh, Nepal, Afghanistan, Iran and Turkey, where the dowry is transferred to the groom by the family of the bride in the form of a heavy amount of cash, cars, houses, furniture and other material things. In many of above-mentioned places and their traditions, this dowry comes under the possession of the groom and the bride has no right to it while in some other places she only inherits this dowry after the death of her husband. In olden times, people had many children both daughters and sons, they used to give dowries to their daughters and they used to be compensated for it by receiving dowries from their daughters in law. But what about a family where one had only daughters? Many parents undergo a lot of stress and as a result thousands have resorted to suicide because they are unable to collect the amount of money and get their daughters married and many today still feel unhappy about giving birth to female children. They feel that these daughters will be a burden on them for the rest of their lives. The mentality of these people is that the better the groom in terms of education or status, the higher his dowry will be. Another issue that rises with this system of giving dowry, is the growing greed of both the groom and his family. Even if the dowry that is paid is significant, they not only demand more and more but also resort to violence and many times even killing. They afflict all sorts of violence where the bride is tortured physically, emotionally and even sexually. This practice does not only come from the places mentioned above but it also has roots from the western as well as the Arab

The Blissful Union ©2017 Syed ISBN 978-93-5268-923-1

world such as United States, Germany, France, many other parts in Europe, Egypt and Morocco. This practice has become a major social evil today, sadly, even amongst many muslims.

Islam, however, gives a very different perspective to dowry. It is a right of the women and it is obligatory upon every muslim man to give, whatever he is able, to his wife as a gift at the time of *Nikah.*

Allah states in Al-Quran (4:4):

وَءَاتُوا۟ ٱلنِّسَآءَ صَدُقَـٰتِهِنَّ نِحْلَةً ۚ فَإِن طِبْنَ لَكُمْ عَن شَىْءٍ مِّنْهُ نَفْسًا فَكُلُوهُ هَنِيٓـًٔا مَّرِيٓـًٔا

"And give to the women (whom you marry) their *Mahr* (obligatory bridal-money given by the husband to his wife at the time of marriage) with a good heart, but if they, of their own good pleasure, remit any part of it to you, take it, and enjoy it without fear of any harm (as Allah has made it lawful)."

And Allah states in Al-Quran (4:20-21):

وَإِنْ أَرَدتُّمُ ٱسْتِبْدَالَ زَوْجٍ مَّكَانَ زَوْجٍ وَءَاتَيْتُمْ إِحْدَىٰهُنَّ قِنطَارًا فَلَا تَأْخُذُوا۟ مِنْهُ شَيْـًٔا ۚ أَتَأْخُذُونَهُۥ بُهْتَـٰنًا وَإِثْمًا مُّبِينًا (٢٠) وَكَيْفَ تَأْخُذُونَهُۥ وَقَدْ أَفْضَىٰ بَعْضُكُمْ إِلَىٰ بَعْضٍ وَأَخَذْنَ مِنكُم مِّيثَـٰقًا غَلِيظًا (٢١)

"If you intend to replace a wife by another and you have given one of them a Qintar (of gold i.e. a great amount as *Mahr*), take not the least bit of it back; would you take it wrongfully without a right and (with) a manifest sin? (20) And how could you take it (back) while you have gone in unto each other, and they have taken from you a firm and strong covenant? (21)."

We also find many *ahadith* regarding the dower

Imam At-Tabrani reported in his *Mu'jam al-Awsat* no.1851 with an authentic chain of narration that Messenger of Allah (ﷺ) said:

أَيُّمَا رَجُلٍ تَزَوَّجَ امْرَأَةً بِمَا قَلَّ مِنَ الْمَهْرِ أَوْ كَثُرَ لَيْسَ فِي نَفْسِهِ أَنْ يُؤَدِّيَ إِلَيْهَا
حَقَّهَا، خَدَعَهَا، فَمَاتَ وَلَمْ يُؤَدِّ إِلَيْهَا حَقَّهَا، لَقِيَ اللَّهَ يَوْمَ الْقِيَامَةِ وَهُوَ زَانٍ

"If one marries a woman on a given dowry and he intends that he will give her nothing, he is considered a deceiver. If he dies without paying her right, he will meet Allah as adulterer on the Day of Judgment."

While Islam states the obligation of giving the dower upon the man, many women misuse this right and demand huge amounts of money. This becomes a cause for other types of evil, where the men who are unable to fulfill these demands, either do not wish to get married and are led to *Haram* relationships or many women from these societies are left unmarried due to their illogical expectations.
Islam also deals with this issue with many instances from the life of the Prophet (ﷺ). One such instance is the dower that was given to his daughter Fatima.

It is reported by Imam Abu Dawood in his *Sunan* no.2125 with an authentic chain of narration:

لَمَّا تَزَوَّجَ عَلِيٌّ فَاطِمَةَ قَالَ لَهُ رَسُولُ اللَّهِ صلى الله عليه وسلم " أَعْطِهَا شَيْئًا " .
" قَالَ مَا عِنْدِي شَىْءٌ . قَالَ أَيْنَ دِرْعُكَ الْحُطَمِيَّةُ

The Blissful Union ©2017 Syed ISBN 978-93-5268-923-1

"When Ali married Fatimah, the Prophet (ﷺ) said to him: Give her something. He said: I have nothing with me. He said: Where is your Hutamiyyah (coat of mail)."

And it is reported by Imam al-Bukhari in his *Saheeh* no.5121

عَنْ سَهْلٍ، أَنَّ امْرَأَةً، عَرَضَتْ نَفْسَهَا عَلَى النَّبِيِّ صلى الله عليه وسلم فَقَالَ لَهُ رَجُلٌ يَا رَسُولَ اللَّهِ زَوِّجْنِيهَا. فَقَالَ " مَا عِنْدَكَ ". قَالَ مَا عِنْدِي شَىْءٌ. قَالَ " اذْهَبْ فَالْتَمِسْ وَلَوْ خَاتَمًا مِنْ حَدِيدٍ ". فَذَهَبَ ثُمَّ رَجَعَ فَقَالَ لاَ وَاللَّهِ مَا وَجَدْتُ شَيْئًا، وَلاَ خَاتَمًا مِنْ حَدِيدٍ، وَلَكِنْ هَذَا إِزَارِي وَلَهَا نِصْفُهُ ـ قَالَ سَهْلٌ وَمَا لَهُ رِدَاءٌ. فَقَالَ النَّبِيُّ صلى الله عليه وسلم " وَمَا تَصْنَعُ بِإِزَارِكَ إِنْ لَبِسْتَهُ لَمْ يَكُنْ عَلَيْهَا مِنْهُ شَىْءٌ، وَإِنْ لَبِسَتْهُ لَمْ يَكُنْ عَلَيْكَ مِنْهُ شَىْءٌ ". فَجَلَسَ الرَّجُلُ حَتَّى إِذَا طَالَ مَجْلَسُهُ قَامَ فَرَآهُ النَّبِيُّ صلى الله عليه وسلم فَدَعَاهُ أَوْ دُعِي لَهُ فَقَالَ " مَاذَا مَعَكَ مِنَ الْقُرْآنِ ". فَقَالَ مَعِي سُورَةُ كَذَا وَسُورَةُ كَذَا لِسُوَرٍ يُعَدِّدُهَا. فَقَالَ النَّبِيُّ صلى الله عليه وسلم " أَمْلَكْنَاكَهَا بِمَا مَعَكَ مِنَ الْقُرْآنِ "

"Narrated Sahl bin Sa`d: A woman presented herself to the Prophet (for marriage). A man said to him, "O Allah's Messenger (ﷺ)! (If you are not in need of her) marry her to me." The Prophet (ﷺ) said, "What have you got?" The man said, "I have nothing." The Prophet (ﷺ) said (to him), "Go and search for something) even if it were an iron ring." The man went and returned saying, "No, I have not found anything, not even an iron ring; but this is my *(Izar)* waist sheet, and half of it is for her." He had no *Rida'* (upper garment). The Prophet (ﷺ) said, "What will she do with your waist sheet? If you wear it, she will have nothing over her; and if she wears it, you will have nothing over you." So the man sat down and when he had sat a long time, he got up (to leave). When the Prophet (ﷺ) saw him (leaving), he called him back, or the man was called (for him), and he said to the man, "How much of the Qur'an do you know (by heart)?" The man replied I know such *Surah* and such *Surah* (by heart)," naming the *Surahs* The Prophet (ﷺ) said, "I have married her to you for what you know of the Qur'an ."

The Blissful Union ©2017 Syed ISBN 978-93-5268-923-1

Marriage without permission of a guardian

Many a time, we hear instances amongst the muslim youth, about girls running away with boys and vice versa and getting married without the permission of their *wali*, sometimes even without the knowledge of their parents and guardians. If they see signs of their guardian's refusal they elope with their partners who, to begin with, are with them in a *haram* relationship such as girlfriend or boyfriend. Those whom they have known for a few months, sometimes years and then decide to get married. They do this in the courts in the same country, city or town and some go to the extent of leaving their place of residence, thinking that this is allowed. They then live with this person having children with them , all this while being unaware that their marriage is invalid. Such cases are not few, In fact, the more you hear about people having illegitimate partners, the more you would hear of such instances.
But know that marriage without a *wali* (male guardian) is invalid.

In *Saheeh Al-Bukhari*, Imam Al-Bukhari brought a chapter in *book of Nikah*

باب من قال لا نكاح إلا بولي

Chapter: Whoever said, "A marriage is not valid except through the *Wali* (Guardian)."

And Imam Al-Bukhari quoted these *ayaat* of Quran in support of this chapter.

فَلَا تَعۡضُلُوهُنَّ أَن يَنكِحۡنَ أَزۡوَٰجَهُنَّ

The Blissful Union ©2017 Syed ISBN 978-93-5268-923-1

"And do not prevent them from marrying their (former) husbands." Al-Quran (2:232).

وَلَا تَنكِحُواْ ٱلْمُشْرِكَٰتِ حَتَّىٰ يُؤْمِنَّ

"And do not marry *Al-Mushrikat* (idolatresses, etc.) till they believe (worship Allah Alone)." Al-Quran (2:221).

وَأَنكِحُواْ ٱلْأَيَٰمَىٰ مِنكُمْ

"And marry off those among you who are single." Al-Quran (24:32).

Imam al-Bukhari wants to prove from these *ayaat* that there should be a guardian in marriage, because Allah is addressing the guardian with regard to the marriage of the woman under his care. If the matter were up to her and not him, there would be no need to address him.

Messenger of Allah (ﷺ) said in an authentic *hadith* reported in *Sunan Abu Dawood* no.2083:

" أَيُّمَا امْرَأَةٍ نَكَحَتْ بِغَيْرِ إِذْنِ مَوَالِيهَا فَنِكَاحُهَا بَاطِلٌ " . ثَلاَثَ مَرَّاتٍ

The marriage of a woman who marries without the consent of her guardian is void (invalid). (He said these words) three times

Imam Ibn Qudamah has narrated an *Ijmaa* (consensus) of scholars in *al-Mughni* (9/358) regarding the order of ranks for one to be the guardian of a woman: And the order is:

1.Father 2.Grandfather (from the father's side) 3.Great Grandfather (from the father's side) 4. Son 5. Grandson 6. Great Grandson 7.Oldest Brother

8. Next Oldest Brother (and so on…) and scholars have ruled that if a lesser-ranking *walee* marries off a woman with the availability of a higher-ranking walee without any valid excuse or without him authorizing it, then such a marriage is invalid.

Shaykhul Islam Ibn Taymiyyah said in *Al-Ikhtiyaraat* (p. 350)

إذا تعذر من له ولاية النكاح انتقلت الولاية إلى أصلح من يوجد ممن له نوع ولاية في غير النكاح كرئيس القرية وأمير القافلة ونحوه

" If there is no relative who can act as her guardian, then the position of guardian passes to the one who is most fit among those who have any kind of authority in matters other than marriage, such as the head of a village, the leader of a caravan, and so on."

The Blissful Union ©2017 Syed ISBN 978-93-5268-923-1

What if the guardian is preventing the woman to marry the suitor of her choice who is suitable for her?

Shaykhul Islam Ibn Taymiyyah said in *Majmoo al Fatawa* (32/52-53):

"And when she is willing to marry a man who is suitable for her, then it is obligatory on her guardian, like the brother then the uncle, that they should marry her with him, and if he (the guardian) stops her from getting married or refrain from it, then according to the agreement of the scholars the next closest relative or the *Haakim* (ruler) will make her *Nikah* (marriage) without the permission of first guardian. It is from the consensus of the scholars that the guardian cannot force her to marry someone she is not willing to marry or to prevent her from marrying someone she is willing to marry if he is suitable for her. Those who prevent her (from getting married where she is willing) and forcing her (to marry other person) are upon the way of oppressors at the time of ignorance, who in their guardianship wanted women to marry whom they choose for her for some personal interests not for her benefit. Then they would force her and make her ashamed until she marries a person of their choice, and they stop her from marrying a suitable person for her due to their enmity or any other purpose. All of this is the practice of the days of al *Jaahiliyah* (ignorance) and oppression and transgression, which is prohibited according to Allah and his Messenger (peace be upon him), and it is prohibited according to the consensus of the scholars. Allah obligates the guardians of women to see the interest of women rather than following their desires, like those guardians who are responsible for other matters, who are given guardianship of those things, they see the benefit of those who are under their guardianship and not that which fulfills their personal desires. Indeed this is the *Amaanah* (trust) which Allah mentioned that it is obligatory to fulfill. "Indeed,

The Blissful Union ©2017 Syed ISBN 978-93-5268-923-1

Allah commands you to render trusts to whom they are due and when you judge between people to judge with justice." (Al-Quran 4:58). This sincerity is obligation as the Messenger of Allah said: "Religion is sincerity, religion is sincerity *(Al-Naseehah)*, religion is sincerity." They said; "To whom, O Messenger of Allah?" He said: "To Allah, to His Book, to His Messenger, to the imams of the Muslims and to their common folk." and Allah knows best."

The Blissful Union ©2017 Syed ISBN 978-93-5268-923-1

The Salaf (pious predecessors) advising their daughters before marriage

It is crucial that parents advice their sons and daughters on marriage before their children get married. Mother needs to advice their sons about the feelings of women and how they could be best dealt with, as the mothers have been wives themselves and they are in better positions to know the needs of a wife and the best ways to deal with them. Likewise, fathers need to advice their daughters on how the needs of their men be fulfilled in the manner prescribed by the *Shareeah*. Doing these will help the young husbands and wives to deal with their spouses better and make it easier for them to make their marriage successful.

Imam Abu Zayd Umar bin Shu'ba narrated in his *Tareekh al-Madeenah* (2/110) with an authentic chain of narration that when Farafasah bin Ahwas married his daughter, Naila, to Uthman bin Affan (May Allah be pleased with him), he advised her saying:

"O my daughter! You are going to people of Quraysh, so pay heed to this advice from me.

1) Use kohl (a substance for lining one's eyes).
2) Take bath frequently and keep yourself clean.
3) Use perfume and smell good."

Imam Salahuddin Khaleel As-Safdi reported an advice of a mother to her daughter before marriage (from pious predecessors) in his book *Al-Wafi bil-Wafayat* (5/309):

"A ruler of Kinda, Amr bin Hajr, proposed Umm Iyaas bint Aouf bin Muslim Ash-Shaybani. When the bride was made ready to be taken to the groom, her mother Umamah advised her daughter stating:

"O my daughter, if a woman were able to do without a husband by virtue of her father's wealth and her need for her father, then you of all people would be most able to do without a husband, but women were created for men and men were created for women.

O my daughter, you are about to leave the home in which you grew up, where you first learned to walk, to go to a place you do not know, to a companion to whom you are unfamiliar. Be like a servant to your husband and he will become like a servant to you.
Inculcate these ten qualities in you and it will be a provision for you.

The first and second of them are: be content in his company for contentment brings peace of mind, listen to and obey him.

The third and fourth of them are: make sure that you smell good and look good; he should not see anything ugly in you, and he should not smell anything but a pleasant smell from you.

The fifth and sixth of them are: prepare his food on time, and keep quiet when he is asleep, for raging hunger is like a burning flame, and disturbing his sleep will make him angry.

The seventh and eighth of them are: take care of his wealth, for taking care of his wealth shows that you appreciate him, and be good to his family and relatives for being good to his family and relatives shows good management.

The Blissful Union ©2017 Syed ISBN 978-93-5268-923-1

The ninth and tenth of them are: never disclose any of his secrets, and never disobey any of his orders, for if you disclose any of his secrets you will never feel safe from his possible betrayal, and if you disobey him, his heart will be filled with hatred towards you."

The Blissful Union ©2017 Syed ISBN 978-93-5268-923-1

Advice from Us

1) *Communication*:

Being able to talk openly with your partner is a sign of a strong marriage. Beware of your tone and the volume of your voice. Your tone determines whether you will make your relationship or break it.

Allah says in Al-Quran (31:19):

وَٱقْصِدْ فِى مَشْيِكَ وَٱغْضُضْ مِن صَوْتِكَ ۚ إِنَّ أَنكَرَ ٱلْأَصْوَٰتِ لَصَوْتُ ٱلْحَمِيرِ

"And be moderate (or show no insolence) in your walking, and lower your voice. Verily, the harshest of all voices is the braying of the ass."

You should be able to communicate with your spouse your needs and wants, and if you dislike something in your spouse that needs to be changed, communicate it in a manner that will not hurt their feelings. There could be two ways in which you might dislike something in your spouse. One is regarding the worldly matters and the other is religious matters. It is better that you overlook the worldly matters unless it reaches a point where it is causing dislike in the your heart regarding your spouse. In this case you can communicate with your spouse openly using wisdom what it is you would like to be changed. If it is a religious matter it is better that it is communicated in a polite manner. If you do not communicate with your spouse what you feel and keep everything in your heart, this builds up anger and resentment which can have negative effects on the relationship. How will your spouse know what you feel if you choose to hide things from them?

The Blissful Union ©2017 Syed ISBN 978-93-5268-923-1

2) *Smile*:

Smiling is a Sunnah of Messenger of Allah (ﷺ). Imam Tirmidhi narrated in his *Jaami at-Tirmidhi* no. 4002 with an authentic chain:

عَبْدِ اللَّهِ بْنِ الْحَارِثِ بْنِ جَزْءٍ، قَالَ مَا رَأَيْتُ أَحَدًا أَكْثَرَ تَبَسُّمًا مِنْ رَسُولِ اللَّهِ صلى الله عليه وسلم

"Narrated Ibn Jaz: I have not seen anyone who smiled more than the Messenger of Allah (ﷺ)."

"The expression one wears on one's face is far more important than the clothes one wears on one's back."

Imam Tirmidhi narrated in his *Jaami at-Tirmidhi* no. 1956 with an authentic chain that Messenger of Allah (ﷺ) said:

تَبَسُّمُكَ فِي وَجْهِ أَخِيكَ لَكَ صَدَقَةٌ

"Your smiling in the face of your brother is charity."

Love is a body where it's soul is the smile. Smiles are so powerful that many marriages have begun with a single smile. When you smile at another person, the physical action releases endorphins in your brain. They make you feel happy and raise your self-esteem. It is upon the wives that they should receive their husbands with a cheerful face. When a man goes out of his home he sees and may come in contact with other women which could be a trial for him. But when he returns home to his wife who receives him in the most pleasant of manner he should feel that he has not seen someone more beautiful than her.

3) *Abstain from argumentation*

Arguments are a normal part of life — it's certainly not expected that you never disagree with the person that you care about. But what can help is finding a way to disagree that doesn't drive a wedge between the two of you.

Imam Abu Dawood reported in his *Sunan* no. 4800 with an authentic chain that Messenger of Allah (ﷺ) said:

" أَنَا زَعِيمٌ بِبَيْتٍ فِي رَبَضِ الْجَنَّةِ لِمَنْ تَرَكَ الْمِرَاءَ وَإِنْ كَانَ مُحِقًّا وَبِبَيْتٍ فِي وَسَطِ الْجَنَّةِ لِمَنْ تَرَكَ الْكَذِبَ وَإِنْ كَانَ مَازِحًا وَبِبَيْتٍ فِي أَعْلَى الْجَنَّةِ لِمَنْ حَسَّنَ خُلُقَهُ "

"I guarantee a house in the surroundings of Paradise for a man who avoids quarreling even if he were in the right, a house in the middle of Paradise for a man who avoids lying even if he were joking, and a house in the upper part of Paradise for a man who made his character good."

4) *Express your affection:*

Keep reminding each other that you love each other and nurture your relationship with kind words. This is done by increasing the use of the statements like "I love you", "I'm here for you", "I cant live without you", "You are so beautiful" , "You are so handsome" and so on. Expressing affection towards your spouse in front of people will increase their love towards you.

Here is an example narrated by Aisha (May Allah be pleased with her) on how Prophet (ﷺ) expressed his love for her.

Imam Al-Bukhari narrated in his *Saheeh* no. 2581:

"From Aisha: The wives of Allah's Messenger (ﷺ) were in two groups. One group consisted of Aisha, Hafsa, Safiyya and Sauda; and the other group consisted of Umm Salama and the other wives of Allah's Messenger (ﷺ). The Muslims knew that Allah's Messenger (ﷺ) loved Aisha, so if any of them had a gift and wished to give to Allah's Messenger (ﷺ), he would delay it, till Allah's Messenger (ﷺ) had come to Aisha's home and then he would send his gift to Allah's Messenger (ﷺ) in her home. The group of Umm Salama discussed the matter together and decided that Umm Salama should request Allah's Messenger (ﷺ) to tell the people to send their gifts to him in whatever wife's house he was. Umm Salama told Allah's Messenger (ﷺ) of what they had said, but he did not reply. Then they (those wives) asked Umm Salama about it. She said, "He did not say anything to me." They asked her to talk to him again. She talked to him again when she met him on her day, but he gave no reply. When they asked her, she replied that he had given no reply. They said to her, "Talk to him till he gives you a reply." When it was her turn, she talked to him again. He then said to her, "Do not hurt me regarding Aisha, as the Divine Inspirations do not come to me on any of the beds except that of Aisha." On that Umm Salama said, "I repent to Allah for hurting you." Then the group of Um Salama called Fatima, the daughter of Allah's Messenger (ﷺ) and sent her to Allah's Messenger (ﷺ) to say to him, "Your wives request to treat them and the daughter of Abu Bakr on equal terms." Then Fatima conveyed the message to him. The Prophet (ﷺ) said, "O my daughter! Don't you love whom I love?" She replied in the affirmative and returned and told them of the situation. They requested her to go to him again but she refused. They then sent Zainab bint Jahsh who went to him and used harsh words saying, "Your wives request you to treat them and the daughter of Ibn Abu Quhafa on equal terms." On that she raised her voice and scolded Aisha to her face so much so that Allah's Messenger (ﷺ) looked at Aisha to see whether she would retort. Aisha started replying to Zainab till she silenced her. The Prophet (ﷺ) then looked at Aisha and said, She is really the daughter of Abu Bakr."

5) *Showing appreciation and gratitude.*

Imam Abu Dawood reported in his *Sunan* no. 4811 with an authentic chain that Messenger of Allah (ﷺ) said:

" لاَ يَشْكُرُ اللَّهَ مَنْ لاَ يَشْكُرُ النَّاسَ "

"He who does not thank the people is not thankful to Allah."

In general we thank others for little courtesies, but do we express gratitude to our partner? Appreciating your spouse is something that strengthens the relationship because it makes us to see how we are appreciated and affirmed by our spouse. Though this is a general advice for both men and women alike, it is more likely that women might show ingratitude to their husbands.

It is reported by Imam Al-Bukhari in his *Saheeh* no.1052 that the Messenger of Allah (ﷺ) said:

" رِأَيتُ النَّارَ، فَلَمْ أَرَ مَنْظَرًا كَالْيَوْمِ قَطُّ أَفْظَعَ، وَرَأَيْتُ أَكْثَرَ أَهْلِهَا النِّسَاءَ ".
قَالُوا بِمَ يَا رَسُولَ اللَّهِ قَالَ " بِكُفْرِهِنَّ ". قِيلَ يَكْفُرْنَ بِاللَّهِ قَالَ " يَكْفُرْنَ
الْعَشِيرَ، وَيَكْفُرْنَ الإِحْسَانَ، لَوْ أَحْسَنْتَ إِلَى إِحْدَاهُنَّ الدَّهْرَ كُلَّهُ، ثُمَّ رَأَتْ
مِنْكَ شَيْئًا قَالَتْ مَا رَأَيْتُ مِنْكَ خَيْرًا قَطُّ ."

“I also saw the Hell-fire and I had never seen such a horrible sight. I saw that most of the inhabitants were women." The people asked, "O Allah's Messenger (ﷺ)! Why is it so?" The Prophet (ﷺ) replied, "Because of their ungratefulness." It was asked whether they are ungrateful to Allah. The Prophet said, "They are ungrateful to their companions of life (husbands) and ungrateful to good deeds. If you are benevolent to one of them throughout the life and if she sees anything (undesirable) in you, she will say, ‘I have never had any good from you.’”

6) *Controlling your anger:*

When one is fire, the other one should be water. Try to control your anger as much as possible with your spouse. Overlook their mistakes and learn to forgive. It is easier to be said than to be done, but one who really applies this in their life will see long lasting positive effects on their relationship. It is said that a man came to see a woman as a prospect for his future wife. Upon being asked by her about his biggest weakness, he replied that his biggest shortcoming is his raging anger. This man was very religious, so she decided that she will agree to marry him despite this characteristic of his. She then narrated that there was something that she did, which after a few years of their marriage, diminished anger in her husband completely. She said that every time her husband got angry, she would take a glass of water, take the water in her mouth without swallowing it so that she wouldn't be able to reply to him.

Even though this might have required a lot of patience to do, but the end result was something very positive. People in anger often do not realize the harshness of their words, that what they say can hurt the receiving person deeply and for a long time. Swallowing anger is from the noble characteristics and it is praised by Allah in the Quran.

Allah says in Al-Quran (3:134):

ٱلَّذِينَ يُنفِقُونَ فِى ٱلسَّرَّآءِ وَٱلضَّرَّآءِ وَٱلْكَـٰظِمِينَ ٱلْغَيْظَ وَٱلْعَافِينَ عَنِ ٱلنَّاسِ ۗ وَٱللَّهُ يُحِبُّ ٱلْمُحْسِنِينَ

"Those who spend [in Allah's Cause] in prosperity and in adversity, who repress anger, and who pardon men; verily, Allah loves *Al-Muhsinun* (the good - doers)."

Imam Al-Bukhari dedicated an entire chapter on this issue in his *Saheeh* named:

باب الْحَذَرِ مِنَ الْغَضَبِ

"Chapter: To be cautious from being angry."

In it he reported a *hadith* no. 6116:

عَنْ أَبِي هُرَيْرَةَ ـ رضى الله عنه ـ أَنَّ رَجُلاً، قَالَ لِلنَّبِيِّ صلى الله عليه وسلم أَوْصِنِي. قَالَ " لاَ تَغْضَبْ ". فَرَدَّدَ مِرَارًا، قَالَ " لاَ تَغْضَبْ ".

"Narrated Abu Huraira: A man said to the Prophet (ﷺ) , "Advise me! "The Prophet (ﷺ) said, "Do not become angry and furious." The man asked (the same) again and again, and the Prophet (ﷺ) said in each case, 'Do not become angry and furious.'"

Hafidh Ibn Rajab explained the above *hadith* in his *Jaami Al-Uloom wal-Hikam* (1/364): "Prophet (ﷺ) is ordering the person to follow the means which will prevent him from getting angry. A person should learn how to change his character and adopt characteristics of kindness, calmness, modesty, patience, forbearance, forgiveness, easy going nature and so on. If a

The Blissful Union ©2017 Syed ISBN 978-93-5268-923-1

person adopts these qualities and he becomes used to such behavior, then it will help him to control his temper when he is angry."

Under same chapter of his *Saheeh* no. 6115, Imam Al-Bukhari brought a narration from the Prophet (ﷺ) where he advised the person who got angry to recite:

أَعُوذُ بِاللَّهِ مِنَ الشَّيْطَانِ الرَّجِيمِ

"I seek refuge with Allah from Satan, the outcast."

Imam Abu Dawood reported in his *Sunan* no. 4782 with an authentic chain that Messenger of Allah (ﷺ) said:

" إِذَا غَضِبَ أَحَدُكُمْ وَهُوَ قَائِمٌ فَلْيَجْلِسْ فَإِنْ ذَهَبَ عَنْهُ الْغَضَبُ وَإِلاَّ فَلْيَضْطَجِعْ "

"When one of you becomes angry while standing, he should sit down. If the anger leaves him, well and good; otherwise he should lie down."

7) *Don't let others come between you and your spouse.*

Sometimes it's a good friend, a beloved family member, or even someone you hardly know. The people from your life can negatively affect your relationship with your spouse. Couples have to work together against any forces that try to break them apart.
Imam Muslim reported in his *Saheeh* no. 2813 that Messenger of Allah (ﷺ) said:

إِنَّ إِبْلِيسَ يَضَعُ عَرْشَهُ عَلَى الْمَاءِ ثُمَّ يَبْعَثُ سَرَايَاهُ فَأَدْنَاهُمْ مِنْهُ مَنْزِلَةً
أَعْظَمُهُمْ فِتْنَةً يَجِيءُ أَحَدُهُمْ فَيَقُولُ فَعَلْتُ كَذَا وَكَذَا فَيَقُولُ مَا صَنَعْتَ شَيْئًا
قَالَ ثُمَّ يَجِيءُ أَحَدُهُمْ فَيَقُولُ مَا تَرَكْتُهُ حَتَّى فَرَّقْتُ بَيْنَهُ وَبَيْنَ امْرَأَتِهِ - قَالَ -
فَيُدْنِيهِ مِنْهُ وَيَقُولُ نِعْمَ أَنْتَ

"*Iblis* (Satan) places his throne upon water; he then sends detachments (for creating dissension) ; the nearer to him in rank are those who are most notorious in creating dissension. One of them comes and says: 'I did so and so.' And he says: 'You have done nothing.' Then one amongst them comes and says: 'I did not spare so and so until I sowed the seed of discord between a husband and a wife.' The Satan goes near him and says: 'You have done well.'"

Permissibility of Singing decent songs in wedding ceremonies

It is permissible to beat *daff* and sing decent songs which is free from immorality during wedding.

Imam Al-Bukhari reported in his *Saheeh* no. 5147,

قَالَتِ الرُّبَيِّعُ بِنْتُ مُعَوِّذٍ ابْنِ عَفْرَاءَ. جَاءَ النَّبِيُّ صلى الله عليه وسلم فَدَخَلَ حِينَ بُنِيَ عَلَىَّ، فَجَلَسَ عَلَى فِرَاشِي كَمَجْلِسِكَ مِنِّي، فَجَعَلَتْ جُوَيْرِيَاتٌ لَنَا يَضْرِبْنَ بِالدُّفِّ وَيَنْدُبْنَ مَنْ قُتِلَ مِنْ آبَائِي يَوْمَ بَدْرٍ، إِذْ قَالَتْ إِحْدَاهُنَّ وَفِينَا نَبِيٌّ يَعْلَمُ مَا فِي غَدٍ. فَقَالَ " دَعِي هَذِهِ، وَقُولِي بِالَّذِي كُنْتِ تَقُولِينَ

"Rubayyi bint Muawwidh bin Afra narrated: After the consummation of my marriage, the Prophet (ﷺ) came and sat on my bed as far from me as you are sitting now, and our little girls started beating the tambourines and reciting elegiac verses mourning my father who had been killed in the battle of Badr. One of them said, 'Among us is a Prophet who knows what will happen tomorrow.' On that the Prophet said, 'Leave this (saying) and keep on saying the verses which you had been saying before.'"

Imam Al-Bukhari narrated in his *Saheeh* no. 5162

عَائِشَةَ، أَنَّهَا زَفَّتِ امْرَأَةً إِلَى رَجُلٍ مِنَ الأَنْصَارِ فَقَالَ نَبِيُّ اللَّهِ صلى الله عليه وسلم " يَا عَائِشَةُ مَا كَانَ مَعَكُمْ لَهْوٌ فَإِنَّ الأَنْصَارَ يُعْجِبُهُمُ اللَّهْوُ " .

"Narrated Aisha that she prepared a lady for a man from the Ansar as his bride and the Prophet said, 'O Aisha! Haven't you got any amusement (during the marriage ceremony) as the Ansar like amusement (songs of children) ?'"

Wedding Night

Drinking milk and offering it to your wife

It is from the Sunnah to drink milk and offer it to your wife during the first night of your wedding.

Imam Ahmad narrated in his *Musnad* no. 27591 with sound chain of narration from Asmaa bint Yazid ibn As-Sakan who said:

فَقَالَتْ: إِنِّي قَيَّنْتُ عَائِشَةَ لِرَسُولِ اللَّهِ صَلَّى اللَّهُ عَلَيْهِ وَسَلَّمَ ثُمَّ جِئْتُهُ، فَدَعَوْتُهُ لِجِلْوَتِهَا، فَجَاءَ، فَجَلَسَ إِلَى جَنْبِهَا، فَأُتِيَ بِعُسٍّ لَبَنٍ، فَشَرِبَ ثُمَّ نَاوَلَهَا النَّبِيُّ صَلَّى اللَّهُ عَلَيْهِ وَسَلَّمَ، فَخَفَضَتْ رَأْسَهَا وَاسْتَحْيَتْ. قَالَتْ أَسْمَاءُ: فَانْتَهَرْتُهَا وَقُلْتُ لَهَا: خُذِي مِنْ يَدِ النَّبِيِّ صَلَّى اللَّهُ عَلَيْهِ وَسَلَّمَ قَالَتْ: فَأَخَذَتْ، فَشَرِبَتْ شَيْئًا، ثُمَّ قَالَ لَهَا النَّبِيُّ صَلَّى اللَّهُ عَلَيْهِ وَسَلَّمَ: «أَعْطِي تِرْبَكِ» قَالَتْ أَسْمَاءُ: فَقُلْتُ: يَا رَسُولَ اللَّهِ، بَلْ خُذْهُ، فَاشْرَبْ مِنْهُ، ثُمَّ نَاوِلْنِيهِ مِنْ يَدِكَ، فَأَخَذَهُ، فَشَرِبَ مِنْهُ، ثُمَّ نَاوَلَنِيهِ، قَالَتْ: فَجَلَسْتُ، ثُمَّ وَضَعْتُهُ عَلَى رُكْبَتِي، ثُمَّ طَفِقْتُ أُدِيرُهُ، وَأَتْبَعُهُ بِشَفَتَيَّ لِأُصِيبَ مِنْهُ مَشْرَبَ النَّبِيِّ صَلَّى اللَّهُ عَلَيْهِ وَسَلَّمَ، ثُمَّ قَالَ لِنِسْوَةٍ عِنْدِي: «نَاوِلِيهِنَّ» فَقُلْنَ: لَا نَشْتَهِيهِ، فَقَالَ النَّبِيُّ صَلَّى اللَّهُ عَلَيْهِ وَسَلَّمَ: «لَا تَجْمَعْنَ جُوعًا وَكَذِبًا» فَهَلْ أَنْتَ مُنْتَهٍ أَنْ تَقُولَ: لَا أَشْتَهِيهِ؟ فَقُلْتُ: أَيْ أُمَّهْ، لَا أَعُودُ أَبَدًا

"I beautified Aisha for Allah's Messenger, then called him to come to see her unveiled. He came, sat next to her, and brought a large cup of milk from which he drank.Then,he offered it to Aisha, but she lowered her head and felt shy. I scolded her and said to her, 'Take from the hand of the Prophet.' She then took it and drank some. Then, the Prophet said to her, 'Give some to your companion.' At that point, I said: 'O Messenger of Allah, rather take it yourself and drink, and then give it to me from your hand.' He took it, drank some, and then offered it to me. I sat down and put it on my knees. Then, I began rotating it and following it with my lips in order that I might hit the spot from which the Prophet had drunk. Then, the Prophet said about some women who were there with me, 'Give them some.' But, they said: ' don't want it.' (i.e., we are not hungry). The Prophet said: We 'Do not combine hunger and fibbing!' Do you abstain from saying: 'I have no appetite for it'? I said: 'O my mother! (A statement of surprise). I will never repeat it again.'"[11]

---

[11] This hadith is hasan li dhatihi as Shahr bin Hawshab is hasan-ul-hadith according to the correct opinion. Shaykh Albani also brought supporting chains for this in his book Adaab Al-Zifaaf.

The Blissful Union ©2017 Syed ISBN 978-93-5268-923-1

Dua to recite by placing your hands on your wife's head.

One should recite this *Dua* by placing hands on wife's head as reported by Imam Abu Dawood in his *Sunan* 2160 with sound chain of narration.

اللَّهُمَّ إِنِّي أَسْأَلُكَ خَيْرَهَا وَخَيْرَ مَا جَبَلْتَهَا عَلَيْهِ وَأَعُوذُ بِكَ مِنْ شَرِّهَا وَمِنْ شَرِّ مَا جَبَلْتَهَا عَلَيْهِ

(Allaahumma innee as'aluka min khairiha wa khairi maa jabaltaha 'alaihi wa a'oodhubika min sharriha wa sharri maa jabaltaha 'alaihi)

"O Allah, I ask You for the good in her, and in the disposition You have given her; I take refuge in You from the evil in her, and in the disposition You have given her."

The Blissful Union ©2017 Syed ISBN 978-93-5268-923-1

Praying of husband and wife together

Imam Abu Bakr Muhammad bin Ibrahim bin Al-Mundhir reported in his book *Al-Awsat fee as-Sunan wal-Ijmaa wal-Ikhtilaaf* no.1936 with an authentic chain of narration:

عَنْ أَبِي سَعِيدٍ مَوْلَى أَبِي أُسَيْدٍ قَالَ: تَزَوَّجْتُ امْرَأَةً فَكَانَ عِنْدِي لَيْلَةَ زِفَافِ امْرَأَتِي نَفَرٌ مِنْ أَصْحَابِ رَسُولِ اللهِ صَلَّى اللهُ عَلَيْهِ وَسَلَّمَ، فَلَمَّا حَضَرَتِ الصَّلَاةُ أَرَادَ أَبُو ذَرٍّ أَنْ يَتَقَدَّمَ فَيُصَلِّيَ فَجَبَذَهُ حُذَيْفَةُ وَقَالَ: رَبُّ الْبَيْتِ أَحَقُّ بِالصَّلَاةِ. فَقَالَ لِأَبِي مَسْعُودٍ: أَكَذَلِكَ؟ قَالَ: نَعَمْ. قَالَ أَبُو سَعِيدٍ: فَتَقَدَّمْتُ فَصَلَّيْتُ بِهِمْ وَأَنَا يَوْمَئِذٍ عَبْدٌ، وَأَمَرَانِي إِذَا أَتَيْتُ بِامْرَأَتِي أَنْ أُصَلِّيَ رَكْعَتَيْنِ، وَأَنْ تُصَلِّيَ خَلْفِي

"From Abu Sa'eed Mawla Abu Usaid who said: I married a lady and it was my wedding night and a group of the companions of Messenger of Allah were present. When it was time for prayer, Abu Dharr stepped forward to pray and Hudhaifa pulled him back and said: it is more befitting that the owner of the house leads in prayer. So he said to Abu Masood: Is it so? He said: Yes. Abu Saeed said: So I stepped forward and led them in prayer though I was a slave. And they commanded me that when I meet my wife that I pray two Rakahs with her, and that she pray behind me."

In the Bedroom

Foreplay

Islam recognizes women's need for affection and foreplay. Women tend to be more romantic than men. They like kind words, they like to be praised and to feel that they are being cared for. Therefore, there is emphasis on this aspect. Islam teaches men how to deal with their wives when it comes to having intercourse; by starting with foreplay. Having intercourse without foreplay is a form of cruelty to women.

Imam Al-Bukhari narrated in his *Saheeh* no.5080:

قالَ سَمِعْتُ جَابِرَ بْنَ عَبْدِ اللَّهِ، رضى الله عنهما يَقُولُ تَزَوَّجْتُ فَقَالَ لِي رَسُولُ اللَّهِ صلى الله عليه وسلم " مَا تَزَوَّجْتَ ". فَقُلْتُ تَزَوَّجْتُ ثَيِّبًا. فَقَالَ " مَا لَكَ وَلِلْعَذَارَى وَلِعَابِهَا ". فَذَكَرْتُ ذَلِكَ لِعَمْرِو بْنِ دِينَارٍ فَقَالَ عَمْرٌو سَمِعْتُ جَابِرَ بْنَ عَبْدِ اللَّهِ يَقُولُ قَالَ لِي رَسُولُ اللَّهِ صلى الله عليه وسلم " هَلاَّ جَارِيَةً تُلاَعِبُهَا وَتُلاَعِبُكَ "

“Narrated Jabir bin Abdullah:When I got married, Allah's Messenger (ﷺ) said to me, "What type of lady have you married?" I replied, "I have married a matron' He said, “Why don't you have a liking for the virgins and for fondling them?" Jabir also said: Allah's Messenger (ﷺ) said, ‘Why didn't you marry a young girl so that you might play with her and she with you?.’”

Hafidh Ibn Hajr said in the explanation of above *hadith* in *Fath Al-Bari* (9/122):

وَفِيهِ إِشَارَةٌ إِلَى مَصِّ لِسَانِهَا وَرَشْفِ شَفَتَيْهَا وَذَلِكَ يَقَعُ عِنْدَ الْمُلَاعَبَةِ وَالتَّقْبِيلِ

“There in an indication in this for sucking her tongue and her lips and that happens during foreplay and kissing.”

One of the common complaints from women is that their husbands are not interested in foreplay, and men complain that their wives are not interested in intercourse. This is because most of these men do not really know about arousal of women.

Allah made men and women physiologically differently. Men are like flare guns when it comes to arousal. They can be turned on instantly. Women are more like pressure cookers. It takes some time for the heat and pressure to build up and once it does you can make things cook better, faster, longer, and more thoroughly simply by adjusting the heat. With women its all about the build up and in order to really get your woman to the highest level of arousal, you need to not only take your time but you need to know what are the spots in order to get the best responses from her.

Using Siwaak or tooth brush and cleaning one's mouth

Imam Muslim reported in his *Saheeh* no. 253

عَنْ عَائِشَةَ، أَنَّ النَّبِيَّ صلى الله عليه وسلم كَانَ إِذَا دَخَلَ بَيْتَهُ بَدَأَ بِالسِّوَاكِ

"Aisha reported: Whenever Allah's Messenger (ﷺ) entered his house, he used tooth-stick first of all."

No one likes bad breath, especially if you are about to lean in and get close for a kiss. According to a recent study from GOSmile, nine out of ten people between the ages of 16 and 40 feel that having bad breath is the worst social mistake you can make.

Some principles of foreplay

1. *Fractionation*: Creating sexual desire requires 'tension' apart from comfort. Fractionation means pulling a girl out of her current state, bringing her back in again, and then pulling her out again before dragging her in once more. Rinse and repeat! it implies that you touch her body parts by enjoying yourself then you suddenly stop and just do something else for a while, like stop touching her or talk about something else. Later you bring her back into intimacy by touching her or kissing her again.

2. *Teasing*: Give her a hint/taste of what's to come but hold back from giving it to her. Women enjoy anticipation.You need to remember that woman like the idea of 'wanting' and 'expecting' what's going to happen.

3. *Understanding*: What turns one woman on may not work on another, and may even change depending on her emotional & mental state. Thus you need to figure out what turns her on and get to know what your wife loves the most. Vary your stimulation and pay attention to how her body responds to your stimulation and adapt accordingly

4. *Immersion*: One needs to focus on the act. You should really be into what you are doing and you should enjoy this entire act. Enjoy it and have fun.

5. *Emotions:* You should have emotional connection with your partner and you should express your feelings to her. You must make love to her emotions as well as her body.

The Blissful Union ©2017 Syed ISBN 978-93-5268-923-1

Important rule for men: don't be self-centered during love-making

Being self-centered during love-making is guaranteed way of making your wife frustrated. Being self-centered during love making is literally what happens when men become so aroused and sexually excited that all they can focus on is getting their own needs satisfied, and as a result, either they totally neglect or they don't pay attention to the needs of their wives. A man whose mindset is developed on satisfying his own needs will never be able to satisfy his wife, which is why you need to discard this mindset completely.

Knowing erogenous zones

According to the research published in *The Journal of Sexual Medicine,* volume 11, Issue 7, published in 8 May 2014, the most erogenous zones other than sexual organs are: lateral breasts (side breasts), areola (the small ring of skin surrounding the nipple), nipples, neck, lips, ears, scalp and forearms. Other erogenous zones include shoulders, back, buttocks and inner thighs.

Breasts and nipples play a major role in sexual arousal. According to research, nipple stimulation sets fireworks off in the same region of the brain that processes sensations from vagina. Kissing, licking and sucking the erogenous zones like lips, neck, ears, breasts, nipples etc is an excellent foreplay which will make your partner ready for intercourse.

The Blissful Union ©2017 Syed ISBN 978-93-5268-923-1

Passionate kissing (kissing the lips) :

Kissing is one of the most evocative behaviors couples exhibit towards each other. It is a wonderful demonstration of romance and intimacy. According to many scientists, saliva contains the sex hormone, testosterone, which triggers libido, thus passionate kissing (i.e., mouth to mouth kissing) will lead to intense sexual experience.

Art of listening to lips (tip for men on passionate kissing)

One of the best ways of kissing is to focus on how is she kissing you. a) The pressure she is exerting as she kisses you . b) The outline boundary and shape of her lips as she kisses you. c) The firmness of her lips when she kisses you. And then replicate the way she kisses you by matching shape of her lips and the pressure she uses.
You can slowly begin to alter your method of kissing and stroke her hairs or caress other parts of her body and pay attention to what she responds most strongly to.

Ears:
According to research published in *Plastic Surgical Nursing* volume 31, ears in women are highly erogenous. Kissing, nibbling and sucking her ears can send a woman's pleasure to very high level. This area is very sensitive to subtle stimulations such as warmth and the movement of air. In fact it is one of the best techniques one can use to give more pleasure to his spouse.

Neck:
Many women say that one of the top erogenous zones is their neck. According to the research published *The Journal of Sexual*

Medicine volume 11, neck is 'super erogenous zone'. Nearly everyone responds to the sternomastoid muscle. It is commonly abbreviated as SCM, which is a paired muscle in the superficial layers of the side of the neck. It is a fairly long narrow band of muscle and it is loaded with all kinds of receptors and nerve endings that you can use to shake your wife's erotic foundations to the core. It is highly sensitive to kissing, licking, nibbling and biting.

Breasts:
According to the same research published in *The Journal of Sexual Medicine* "nipple stimulation is erotogenic, because it stimulates the same area as the genitals." There is no specific tip which will work on every woman. Some women want breast stimulation in the form of tender, soft teasing, and some want it rougher. Communication and discussing what she likes is very important.

The Blissful Union ©2017 Syed ISBN 978-93-5268-923-1

Satisfying your wife during intercourse

It is important to satisfy the needs of your woman during intercourse. If you finish before her, then wait until she climaxes.

Messenger of Allah (ﷺ) said in an authentic *hadith* reported by Imam Al-Bukhari in his *Saheeh* no.13 and Imam Muslim in his *Saheeh* no.45:

لَا يُؤْمِنُ أَحَدُكُمْ حَتَّى يُحِبَّ لِأَخِيهِ مَا يُحِبُّ لِنَفْسِهِ

"None of you [truly] believes until he loves for his brother that which he loves for himself."

Imam Ibn Qudamah said in his book *Al-Mughni* (8/136):

فإن فرغ قبلَها : كُره له النزع حتى تفرغ

"If he finishes before she does, it is not right for him to withdraw until she finishes."

Women who aren't getting their intimacy needs met by their husbands are most likely to look for it elsewhere, trying to meet their unmet needs through illegitimate sexual relationships. According to one survey, 65% of women who admitted to committing adultery said that they lacked sexual intimacy, so they chose to look for it elsewhere.

Knowing anatomy of the female private part

Understanding the basic functions of the female sex organs is the first huge step to understand how to satisfy woman. In fact it has been reported that many couples did not have intercourse even months after their wedding because husbands did not know where the vagina was located.

Famous scholar of *Tafseer,* Imam al-Qurtubi, explains the anatomy of female sexual organ in explanation of the *ayah* no.23 of *Surah al-Baqarah*. He said in his *Tafseer Qurtubi* (3/95):

وَقَالَ ابْنُ الْعَرَبِيِّ فِي قَبَسِهِ: قَالَ لَنَا الشَّيْخُ الْإِمَامُ فَخْرُ الْإِسْلَامِ أَبُو بَكْرٍ مُحَمَّدُ بْنُ أَحْمَدَ بْنِ الْحُسَيْنِ فَقِيهُ الْوَقْتِ وَإِمَامُهُ: الْفَرْجُ أشبه شي بِخَمْسَةٍ وَثَلَاثِينَ، وَأَخْرَجَ يَدَهُ عَاقِدًا بِهَا. وَقَالَ: مَسْلَكُ الْبَوْلِ مَا تَحْتَ الثَّلَاثِينَ، وَمَسْلَكُ الذَّكَرِ وَالْفَرْجِ مَا اشْتَمَلَتْ عَلَيْهِ الْخَمْسَةُ

And Ibn al-Arabi (famous scholar, author of *Tafseer* and many other books on *fiqh* and explanation of *hadith*) said: *Ash-Shaykh, Al-Imam*, Pride of Islam, Abu Bakr Muhammad bin Ahmad bin Al-Husayn, *Faqeeh* (jurist) and leader of his time said to us: The female sexual organ is the closest to the number 35, then he took out his hand to explain to them (he held his thumb and index finger in a round shape as it is in the 5 and the other three fingers above the index finger as the 3 in 35) and said, 'The path where the urine comes from is what is under the 3 (fingers) and the part where penetration occurs in the round shape (the 5)'.

We have given a brief explanation of the female sexual organ from the scientific point of view below:

Labia Majora:

Labia Majora are the two outer lips of the vaginal opening, and are situated on each side of it, with the labia minora and vaginal opening nested between them. The labium majora are generally covered with pubic hair, unless they have been waxed or shaven.

Labia Minora:

Labia Minora are the two inner lips and are situated on each side of the vaginal opening, and is slightly covered by the labia majora.

Clitoris:

Clitoris is sometimes referred to as "the female penis" or "the love button". It is the little hooded nubbin above the opening of the vagina scientists call "the clitoral glans".The clitoral glans is the only part of the clitoris you can see, but it's actually just the tip. In fact, approximately three quarters of the clitoris is actually inside the body

Clitoris is the human female's most sensitive erogenous zone and generally the primary anatomical source of human female sexual pleasure and sexual stimulation of the clitoris can produce female sexual arousal and orgasm as explained by Carroll and Janell in their research journal *"Sexuality Now: Embracing Diversity"* page 110-111 published in 2012.

The clitoris is similar to the penis, in that it becomes erect during stimulation as mentioned by Kenneth Saladin in *"Human anatomy"* page 738, published in 2010.

Vagina

Vagina is a muscular and tubular part of the female genital tract. Below the opening of the urethra (place from where

The Blissful Union ©2017 Syed ISBN 978-93-5268-923-1

urine is passed out of the body) is the vaginal opening. The vaginal wall can be divided into two parts:
1) High Sensitivity Area, situated near the entrance of the the vaginal opening, and
2) Lower Sensitivity Area, i.e., any area above the high sensitivity area within the vagina.

Perinium:
Perineum is the area just between the anus and the bottom of the outer labia.

It is important to note that all the areas mentioned above are highly sensitive to touch and stimulating them leads to arousal and climax in women. There are different ways of stimulating clitoris like direct stimulation, indirect stimulation. Massaging outer and inner lips of vagina is also great stimulation. Communication with your wife is the best way to find what makes her feel good.

The Blissful Union ©2017 Syed ISBN 978-93-5268-923-1

Stages to achieve female sexual climax

Woman achieving climax has lots of benefits physically, mentally and emotionally. Statistics from various surveys suggests that only 25 percent of all women reach climax during intercourse. According to research of Carol Rinkleib Ellison in the year 2000, reaching climax relieves tension as oxytocin stimulates feelings of warmth and relaxation, and when women experience climax, the amygdala, the part of the brain associated with fear and anxiety, shows little to no activity. According to a new study published in *the journal Cephalalgia*, reaching climax help relieve pain from migraines and cluster headaches.

Here are the stages of female orgasm based on research of Beverly Whipple and Karen Brash- McGreer along with research of Rosemary Basson with slight changes.

1. *Desire:*

One of the primary step in achieving female sexual climax is an attraction. Woman should be sexually attracted to her husband and should desire him.

2. *Excitement:*

To achieve excitement, a woman should be relaxed mentally and physically. Lighting the candles for romantic bedroom, scents and perfumes, relaxing hot bath or sensual massage is helpful in this.

3. *Arousal:*

Foreplay and its principles mentioned above should be applied and stimulation of erogenous zones will lead to this phase. At this stage sexual tension affects the whole body as muscles begin to contract. Women may breathe more quickly or experience little shivers. Nipples may become erect and hard, and a flush or rash may appear on the skin.

4. *Plateau:*

After stimulation of secondary erogenous zones as covered in foreplay, stimulation of primary erogenous zones like labia majora, then labia minora and then clitoris will lead to this stage. The responses may continue to intensify as the vagina becomes more sensitive and the glans of the clitoris retracts under the hood.

5. *Orgasm*:

With enough stimulation of or around the clitoris or intercourse and for some women, pressure on the cervix or other sensitive areas such as the *Grafenberg spot*[12], a woman may build up to a peak, or orgasm. This is the point at which all the tension suddenly releases in a series of involuntary and pleasurable muscular contractions. Contractions may be felt in the vagina, uterus, and rectum. Some women experience orgasm as a total-body contraction and release.

6. *Resolution:*

---

12 The Grafenberg Spot is an area on the forward wall of the vagina, just behind the pubic bone about two inches in. It often feels more "ridged" than the surrounding tissue. Pressing into it can be intensely pleasurable, but may cause a sensation of needing to urinate.

The Blissful Union ©2017 Syed ISBN 978-93-5268-923-1

Unless stimulation continues, the resolution stage occurs. During the half hour or more after orgasm, the muscles relax, and the clitoris, vagina, and uterus return to their usual positions

The Blissful Union ©2017 Syed ISBN 978-93-5268-923-1

Important advice for women regarding intimacy

A wife has to learn and know how to please her husband sexually. Men are visual creatures. It is very easy for them to be aroused by what they see. Many women do not make the effort or take the time to arouse their husbands before moving into intercourse. The following are a few tips a woman can apply in turning her husband on.

1. Make effort: First and foremost, your husband would love to see you make some effort in looking pleasing to him. Men are visual creatures so find out what and how he likes you to be dressed. Remember, the only person you can show every part of your body to is your spouse, so dress as you please to arouse him. Use everything you think he would love to see on you, different types of clothing, the way you do your hair, putting on some makeup and using scents and perfumes that he loves. Do as much as you can to get him in the mood. If you're not sure what he likes don't feel shy asking him.

2. Atmosphere: Set up the atmosphere to make things romantic by lighting some candles or using flowers. Choose what suits you and your husband best.

3. Men love variety: Try new things and ways to please him whether it be different positions, change the place if you can or you can even try giving him a massage once in a while. Do not stick to one same routine as they tend to get bored easily.

4. Be involved in bed: Men like to see that their women are involved and interested in what is going on. Don't be shy to

The Blissful Union ©2017 Syed ISBN 978-93-5268-923-1

show him that you are enjoying the act. They like to see that their wife is enjoying every act.

5. Be confident: This is a thing most women lack! Confidence. You might think what does this have to do with intimacy. Women are usually unhappy with the way they look. They constantly complain about their built or the shape of body so they feel that they will look unattractive to their husbands. This is sometimes increased by comments husbands make. But the lesser confidence you show, the more your man will start to lose interest in being intimate with you. Men love women who show confidence. Also, such insecurities lead to the act of intimacy to not be achieved successfully.

The Blissful Union ©2017 Syed ISBN 978-93-5268-923-1

Coming unto your wife

It is permissible for a Muslim man to enter his wife in her vagina from any direction he wishes.

Allah says in Al-Quran (2:223) :

نِسَآؤُكُمۡ حَرۡثٞ لَّكُمۡ فَأۡتُواْ حَرۡثَكُمۡ أَنَّىٰ شِئۡتُمۡۖ وَقَدِّمُواْ لِأَنفُسِكُمۡۚ وَٱتَّقُواْ ٱللَّهَ وَٱعۡلَمُوٓاْ
أَنَّكُم مُّلَٰقُوهُۗ وَبَشِّرِ ٱلۡمُؤۡمِنِينَ

"Your wives are a tilth for you, so go to your tilth, when or how you will, and send (good deeds, or ask Allah to bestow upon you pious offspring) for your own selves beforehand. And fear Allah, and know that you are to meet Him (in the Hereafter), and give good tidings to the believers."

Imam al-Bukhari reported in his *Saheeh* in book of *Tafseer* no.4528:

سَمِعْتُ جَابِرًا ـ رضى الله عنه ـ قَالَ كَانَتِ الْيَهُودُ تَقُولُ إِذَا جَامَعَهَا مِنْ
وَرَائِهَا جَاءَ الْوَلَدُ أَحْوَلَ. فَنَزَلَتْ {نِسَاؤُكُمْ حَرْثٌ لَكُمْ فَأْتُوا حَرْثَكُمْ أَنَّى شِئْتُمْ}

"Narrated Jabir: Jews used to say: "If one has sexual intercourse with his wife from the back, then she will deliver a squint-eyed child." So this Verse was revealed:-- Your wives are a tilth unto you; so go to your tilth when or how you will."

The above *ayah* indicates the permissibility for the man to enter his wife and have intercourse with her in any position they desire. In fact, this would make intercourse in one's marital life more pleasurable and non-monotonous. Some of the most common positions include man on top, woman on top, sideways, spooning, rear-entry (inside vagina not anus) etc.

Dua to recite before sexual intercourse

Imam al-Bukhari reported in his *Saheeh* in the *Book of Nikah*, no. 5165 that Prophet (ﷺ) said:

أَمَا لَوْ أَنَّ أَحَدَهُمْ يَقُولُ حِينَ يَأْتِي أَهْلَهُ بِاسْمِ اللَّهِ، اللَّهُمَّ جَنِّبْنِي الشَّيْطَانَ، وَجَنِّبِ الشَّيْطَانَ مَا رَزَقْتَنَا، ثُمَّ قُدِّرَ بَيْنَهُمَا فِي ذَلِكَ، أَوْ قُضِيَ وَلَدٌ، لَمْ يَضُرَّهُ شَيْطَانٌ أَبَدًا "

"If anyone of you, when having sexual intercourse with his wife, says: '*Bismillah, Allahumma jannibni-Sh-Shaitan wa jannib-ish-Shaitan ma razaqtana*' (In the name of Allah, O Allah, keep us away from the Satan, and keep the Satan away from that which You may grant us i.e., offspring) and if it is destined that they should have a child, then Satan will never be able to harm him."

Prohibition of Sodomy

Sodomy is anal copulation which is prohibited in Islam. It is major sin for a man to have anal intercourse with his wife.

Allah states in Al-Quran (2:223):

نِسَآؤُكُمْ حَرْثٌ لَّكُمْ فَأْتُوا۟ حَرْثَكُمْ أَنَّىٰ شِئْتُمْ

"Your wives are a tilth for you, so go to your tilth, when or how you will."

The Prophet (ﷺ) explained this Ayah as reported by Imam Muslim in his *Saheeh* no. 1435:

إِنْ شَاءَ مُجَبِّيَةً وَإِنْ شَاءَ غَيْرَ مُجَبِّيَةٍ غَيْرَ أَنَّ ذَلِكَ فِي صِمَامٍ وَاحِدٍ

> "If he likes he may (have intercourse) being on the back or in front of her, but it should be through one opening (vagina)."

The above *hadith* is the evidence that intercourse is allowed through only one opening as mentioned in the above *hadith* and the prophet (ﷺ) has cursed those men who come unto their wives from her anal passage and that Allah will not even look at such a man.

It is reported in *Sunan Abu Dawood* no.2162 with a sound chain of narration:

قَالَ رَسُولُ اللَّهِ صلى الله عليه وسلم "مَلْعُونٌ مَنْ أَتَى امْرَأَتَهُ فِي دُبُرِهَا"

"The Prophet (ﷺ) said: He who has intercourse with his wife through her anus is accursed."
It is reported in *Sunan Ibn Majah* no.1998 with an authentic chain of narration:

عَنْ أَبِي هُرَيْرَةَ، عَنِ النَّبِيِّ - صلى الله عليه وسلم - قَالَ " لاَ يَنْظُرُ اللَّهُ إِلَى رَجُلٍ جَامَعَ امْرَأَتَهُ فِي دُبُرِهَا

"It was narrated from Abu Hurairah: that the Prophet (ﷺ) said: Allah will not look at a man who has intercourse with his wife in her buttocks."

This sin of having intercourse from the anal passage is abhorred in Islam to such an extent that it is equated to disbelief.

It is reported in *Jami At Tirmidhi* no.135 with a sound chain of narration:

عَنِ النَّبِيِّ صلى الله عليه وسلم قَالَ " مَنْ أَتَى حَائِضًا أَوِ امْرَأَةً فِي دُبُرِهَا أَوْ كَاهِنًا فَقَدْ كَفَرَ بِمَا أُنْزِلَ عَلَى مُحَمَّدٍ صلى الله عليه وسلم " .

The Prophet (ﷺ) said: "Whoever engages in sexual intercourse with a menstruating woman, or a woman in her anus, consults a soothsayer, then he has disbelieved in what was revealed to Muhammad."

Kegel exercises for better sex life

According to the study by Anderson RU and team published in *The Journal of Urology* in 2006 , Kegel exercises significantly help in increasing libido and controlling ejaculation.Thus it helps to last longer in bed.

Kegel exercises are directed to strengthen PC muscle.There is a muscle that plays a crucial role in the functioning of the penis called the *pubococcygeus* muscle. The *pubococcygeus* muscle-or PC muscle, for short-is actually a group of muscles that run from the pubic bone to the tailbone. The PC muscle is the muscle you use to stop the flow of urine from the bladder. It is also the muscle that contracts when you ejaculate, moving the semen up through the penis and out of the body. To Locate PC, gently place one or two fingers right behind your testicles. Pretend that you are urinating. Now try to stop the flow. That muscle you just used to turn off the flow from the bladder is your PC muscle. Did you feel it tightening? There are various exercises available and books have been written on this. Interested reader may read those books.

Intercourse with wife during menstruation

It is *haram* to have intercourse with your wife during her period of menstruation.
Allah says in Al-Quran (2:222):

وَيَسْـَٔلُونَكَ عَنِ ٱلْمَحِيضِ ۖ قُلْ هُوَ أَذًى فَٱعْتَزِلُوا۟ ٱلنِّسَآءَ فِى ٱلْمَحِيضِ ۖ وَلَا تَقْرَبُوهُنَّ حَتَّىٰ يَطْهُرْنَ ۖ فَإِذَا تَطَهَّرْنَ فَأْتُوهُنَّ مِنْ حَيْثُ أَمَرَكُمُ ٱللَّهُ ۚ إِنَّ ٱللَّهَ يُحِبُّ ٱلتَّوَّٰبِينَ وَيُحِبُّ ٱلْمُتَطَهِّرِينَ

"They ask you concerning menstruation. Say: that is an *Adha* (a harmful thing for a husband to have a sexual intercourse with his wife while she is having her menses), therefore keep away from women during menses and go not unto them till they are purified (from menses and have taken a bath). And when they have purified themselves, then go in unto them as Allah has ordained for you (go in unto them in any manner as long as it is in their vagina). Truly, Allah loves those who turn unto Him in repentance and loves those who purify themselves (by taking a bath and cleaning and washing thoroughly their private parts, bodies, for their prayers)."

It is reported in *Jami At Tirmidhi* no. 135 with a sound chain of narration:

عَنِ النَّبِيِّ صلى الله عليه وسلم قَالَ " مَنْ أَتَى حَائِضًا أَوِ امْرَأَةً فِي دُبُرِهَا أَوْ كَاهِنًا فَقَدْ كَفَرَ بِمَا أُنْزِلَ عَلَى مُحَمَّدٍ صلى الله عليه وسلم " .

"The Prophet (ﷺ) said: Whoever engages in sexual intercourse with a menstruating woman, or a woman in her anus, consults a soothsayer, then he has disbelieved in what was revealed to Muhammad."

What is permissible to do when woman is in menstruation?

Even though intercourse is not allowed with your wife during menstruation, it is permissible for a husband to enjoy his wife in other ways as stated by the Messenger of Allah (ﷺ).

It is reported in *Sunan Abu Dawood* no.272 with an authentic chain of narration

عَنْ عِكْرِمَةَ، عَنْ بَعْضِ، أَزْوَاجِ النَّبِيِّ صلى الله عليه وسلم أَنَّ النَّبِيَّ صلى الله عليه وسلم كَانَ إِذَا أَرَادَ مِنَ الْحَائِضِ شَيْئًا أَلْقَى عَلَى فَرْجِهَا ثَوْبًا .

"Ikrimah reported on the authority of one of the wives of the Prophet (ﷺ) saying: When the Prophet (ﷺ) wanted to do something (i.e. kissing, embracing) with (his) menstruating wife, he would put a garment on her private part."

Do everything except intercourse

It is reported in *Saheeh Muslim* no. 302:

عَنْ أَنَسٍ، أَنَّ الْيَهُودَ، كَانُوا إِذَا حَاضَتِ الْمَرْأَةُ فِيهِمْ لَمْ يُؤَاكِلُوهَا وَلَمْ يُجَامِعُوهُنَّ فِي الْبُيُوتِ فَسَأَلَ أَصْحَابُ النَّبِيِّ صلى الله عليه وسلم النَّبِيَّ صلى الله عليه وسلم فَأَنْزَلَ اللَّهُ تَعَالَى { وَيَسْأَلُونَكَ عَنِ الْمَحِيضِ قُلْ هُوَ أَذًى فَاعْتَزِلُوا النِّسَاءَ فِي الْمَحِيضِ} إِلَى آخِرِ الآيَةِ فَقَالَ رَسُولُ اللَّهِ صلى الله عليه وسلم " اصْنَعُوا كُلَّ شَىْءٍ إِلاَّ النِّكَاحَ " . فَبَلَغَ ذَلِكَ الْيَهُودَ فَقَالُوا مَا يُرِيدُ هَذَا الرَّجُلُ أَنْ يَدَعَ مِنْ أَمْرِنَا شَيْئًا إِلاَّ خَالَفَنَا فِيهِ فَجَاءَ أُسَيْدُ بْنُ حُضَيْرٍ وَعَبَّادُ بْنُ بِشْرٍ فَقَالاَ يَا رَسُولَ اللَّهِ إِنَّ الْيَهُودَ تَقُولُ كَذَا وَكَذَا . فَلاَ نُجَامِعُهُنَّ فَتَغَيَّرَ وَجْهُ رَسُولِ اللَّهِ صلى الله عليه وسلم حَتَّى ظَنَنَّا أَنْ قَدْ وَجَدَ عَلَيْهِمَا فَخَرَجَا فَاسْتَقْبَلَهُمَا هَدِيَّةٌ مِنْ لَبَنٍ إِلَى النَّبِيِّ صلى الله عليه وسلم فَأَرْسَلَ فِي آثَارِهِمَا فَسَقَاهُمَا فَعَرَفَا أَنْ لَمْ يَجِدْ عَلَيْهِمَا .

"Anas narrated: Among the Jews, when a woman menstruated, they did not dine with her, nor did they live with them in their houses; so the Companions of the Apostle (ﷺ) asked The Apostle (ﷺ), and Allah, the Exalted revealed:" And they ask you about menstruation; say it is a pollution, so keep away from woman during menstruation" to the end (Al-Qur'an 2:222). The Messenger of Allah (ﷺ) said: Do everything except intercourse. The Jews heard of that and said: This man does not want to leave anything we do without opposing us in it. Usaid bin Hudair and Abbad bin Bishr came and said: Messenger of Allah, the Jews say such and such thing. We should not have, therefore, any contact with them (as the Jews do). The face of the Messenger of Allah (way peace be upon him) underwent such a change that we

The Blissful Union ©2017 Syed ISBN 978-93-5268-923-1

thought he was angry with them, but when they went out, they happened to receive a gift of milk which was sent to the Messenger of Allah (ﷺ). He (Prophet) called for them and gave them drink, whereby they knew that he was not angry with them."

Expiation for the one who has intercourse during menses

If a man indulges in intercourse with his wife during her menstruation, then it is upon him to repent to Allah and give expiation for this sin.

Imam Nasa'ee reported in *Sunan* no.370 with an authentic chain of narration

عَنِ ابْنِ عَبَّاسٍ، عَنِ النَّبِيِّ صلى الله عليه وسلم فِي الرَّجُلِ يَأْتِي امْرَأَتَهُ وَهِيَ حَائِضٌ يَتَصَدَّقُ بِدِينَارٍ أَوْ بِنِصْفِ دِينَارٍ

It was narrated from Ibn 'Abbas from the Prophet (ﷺ) concerning a man who has had intercourse with his wife while she was menstruating: "Let him give a Dinar or half a Dinar in charity."
One Dinar is equivalent to 4.25 grams of gold.

When to have sex after menses?

Allah says in Al-Quran (2:222):

وَلَا تَقْرَبُوهُنَّ حَتَّىٰ يَطْهُرْنَ ۖ فَإِذَا تَطَهَّرْنَ فَأْتُوهُنَّ مِنْ حَيْثُ أَمَرَكُمُ ٱللَّهُ

"And go not unto them till they are purified (from menses and have taken a bath). And when they have purified themselves, then go in unto them as Allah has ordained for you (go in unto them in any manner as long as it is in their vagina)."

It is permissible to have intercourse after she washes the place where the blood had been when the flow of blood stops completely and take complete bath (*Ghusl*).

Permissibility of being naked in front of your spouse

Many people hold the misconception that is not allowed to be naked in front of your spouse. It is no where in Islam considered a sin. Rather, these people hold this view either due to their culture or due to baseless *fiqhi* opinions which are based on weak and fabricated narrations.

Imam Abu Dawood narrated in his *Sunan* no. 4017 with sound chain of narration:

بَهْزِ بْنِ حَكِيمٍ، عَنْ أَبِيهِ، عَنْ جَدِّهِ، قَالَ قُلْتُ يَا رَسُولَ اللَّهِ عَوْرَاتُنَا مَا نَأْتِي مِنْهَا وَمَا نَذَرُ قَالَ " احْفَظْ عَوْرَتَكَ إِلاَّ مِنْ زَوْجَتِكَ أَوْ مَا مَلَكَتْ يَمِينُكَ " . قَالَ قُلْتُ يَا رَسُولَ اللَّهِ إِذَا كَانَ الْقَوْمُ بَعْضُهُمْ فِي بَعْضٍ قَالَ " إِنِ اسْتَطَعْتَ أَنْ لاَ يَرَيَنَّهَا أَحَدٌ فَلاَ يَرَيَنَّهَا " . قَالَ قُلْتُ يَا رَسُولَ اللَّهِ إِذَا كَانَ أَحَدُنَا خَالِيًا قَالَ " اللَّهُ أَحَقُّ أَنْ يُسْتَحْيَا مِنْهُ مِنَ النَّاسِ "

"Bahz b. Hakim said that his father told on the authority of his grandfather: I said: Messenger of Allah, from whom should we conceal our private parts and to whom can we show? He replied: conceal your private parts except from your wife and from whom your right hands possess (slave-girls).
I then asked: Messenger of Allah, (what should we do), if the people are assembled together? He replied: If it is within your power that no one looks at it, then no one should look at it.
I then asked: Messenger of Allah if one of us is alone, (what should he do)? He replied: Allah is more entitled than people that bashfulness should be shown to him."

It is preferable to take bath or perform ablution before sleeping or having another sexual intercourse

Imam Abu Dawood narrated in his *Sunan* no.219 with sound chain of narration:

عنْ أَبِي رَافِعٍ، أَنَّ النَّبِيَّ صلى الله عليه وسلم طَافَ ذَاتَ يَوْمٍ عَلَى نِسَائِهِ يَغْتَسِلُ عِنْدَ هَذِهِ وَعِنْدَ هَذِهِ . قَالَ فَقُلْتُ لَهُ يَا رَسُولَ اللَّهِ أَلاَ تَجْعَلُهُ غُسْلاً وَاحِدًا قَالَ " هَذَا أَزْكَى وَأَطْيَبُ وَأَطْهَرُ

"Narrated Abu Rafi: One day the Prophet (ﷺ) had intercourse with all his wives. He took a bath after each intercourse. I asked him: Messenger of Allah, why don't you make it a single bath? He replied: This is more purifying, better and cleaning."

Imam Muslim narrated in his *Saheeh* under chapter:

باب جَوَازِ نَوْمِ الْجُنُبِ وَاسْتِحْبَابِ الْوُضُوءِ لَهُ وَغَسْلِ الْفَرْجِ إِذَا أَرَادَ أَنْ يَأْكُلَ أَوْ يَشْرَبَ أَوْ يَنَامَ أَوْ يُجَامِعَل

"Chapter: It is permissible for one who is *junub* to sleep, but it is recommended for him to perform *wudu* (ablution) , and wash his private parts if he wants to eat, drink, sleep, or have intercourse", no. 305:

عنْ عَائِشَةَ، قَالَتْ كَانَ رَسُولُ اللَّهِ صلى الله عليه وسلم إِذَا كَانَ جُنُبًا فَأَرَادَ أَنْ يَأْكُلَ أَوْ يَنَامَ تَوَضَّأَ وُضُوءَهُ لِلصَّلاَةِ .

"Aisha reported: Whenever the Messenger of Allah (ﷺ) had sexual intercourse and intended to eat or sleep, he performed the ablution of prayer."

Imam Muslim reported under the same chapter no. 308, in his *Saheeh:*

عن أَبِي سَعِيدٍ الْخُدْرِيِّ، قَالَ قَالَ رَسُولُ اللَّهِ صلى الله عليه وسلم " إِذَا أَتَى أَحَدُكُمْ أَهْلَهُ ثُمَّ أَرَادَ أَنْ يَعُودَ فَلْيَتَوَضَّأْ

"Abu Said al-Khudri reported: The Messenger of Allah (ﷺ) said: When anyone amongst you has sexual intercourse with his wife and then he intends to repeat it, he should perform ablution."

The Blissful Union ©2017 Syed ISBN 978-93-5268-923-1

Husband and wife bathing together

Imam Muslim narrated in his *Saheeh* no.321:

عَنْ عَائِشَةَ، قَالَتْ كُنْتُ أَغْتَسِلُ أَنَا وَرَسُولُ اللَّهِ، صلى الله عليه وسلم مِنْ إِنَاءٍ - بَيْنِي وَبَيْنَهُ - وَاحِدٍ فَيُبَادِرُنِي حَتَّى أَقُولَ دَعْ لِي دَعْ لِي . قَالَتْ وَهُمَا جُنُبَانِ .

"Aisha reported: I and the Messenger of Allah (ﷺ) took a bath from one vessel which was placed between me and him and he would get ahead of me, so that I would say: Spare (some water for) me, spare (some water for) me; and she said that they were in a state of sexual impurity."

Imam al-Bukhari narrated in his *Saheeh* no.253:

عَنِ ابْنِ عَبَّاسٍ، أَنَّ النَّبِيَّ صلى الله عليه وسلم وَمَيْمُونَةَ كَانَا يَغْتَسِلاَنِ مِنْ إِنَاءٍ وَاحِدٍ

"Narrated Ibn Abbas: The Prophet (ﷺ) and Maimuna used to take a bath from a single pot."

Some benefits of the bathing of husband and wife together

Bathing with your spouse can bring many benefits in the relationship rather than hurrying through a shower by yourself to become clean. This can boost romance between couples. Even though very simple, the feeling of warm water, soaps and scents can set up the mood for a more wonderful experience. It can bring down stress level, increase love for each other while fostering better communication. Couples can try making it more exciting by filling up the tub with warm water and using scents and soap and sit together in it while enjoying each other.

The Blissful Union ©2017 Syed ISBN 978-93-5268-923-1

Permissibility of condoms and coitus interruptus

Imam al-Bukhari narrated in his *Saheeh* no.5209:

عَنْ جَابِرٍ، قَالَ كُنَّا نَعْزِلُ عَلَى عَهْدِ النَّبِيِّ صلى الله عليه وسلم وَالْقُرْآنُ يَنْزِلُ.

"Jabir narrated: We used to practice coitus interruptus during the lifetime of Allah's Messenger (ﷺ) while the Qur'an was being revealed."

The above *hadith* is evidence for the permissibility of using methods such as *coitus interruptus*[13] and deriving from it the using of condoms but even though its permissible, scholars deem this to be disliked as it negates one of the purpose of marriage which is to reproduce and maintaining human race. Hence, it is upon the husband and wife to weigh the benefits and disadvantages and then base their decision.

[13] It is the practice of withdrawing the penis from the vagina and away from a woman's external genitals before ejaculation to prevent pregnancy. The goal of the withdrawal method is to prevent sperm from entering the vagina.

There is reward if one has intercourse with his wife to keep him chaste

The protection of man's chastity has been given great significance in Islam. A person falls into major sin by committing illicit sexual intercourse, similarly, he is rewarded when he has relations with his wife to keep himself chaste and to protect himself from falling into *haram*.

Imam Muslim narrated in his *Saheeh* no. 1006:

عَنْ أَبِي، ذَرٍّ أَنَّ نَاسًا، مِنْ أَصْحَابِ النَّبِيِّ صلى الله عليه وسلم قَالُوا لِلنَّبِيِّ صلى الله عليه وسلم يَا رَسُولَ اللَّهِ ذَهَبَ أَهْلُ الدُّثُورِ بِالأُجُورِ يُصَلُّونَ كَمَا نُصَلِّي وَيَصُومُونَ كَمَا نَصُومُ وَيَتَصَدَّقُونَ بِفُضُولِ أَمْوَالِهِمْ . قَالَ " أَوَلَيْسَ قَدْ جَعَلَ اللَّهُ لَكُمْ مَا تَصَّدَّقُونَ إِنَّ بِكُلِّ تَسْبِيحَةٍ صَدَقَةً وَكُلِّ تَكْبِيرَةٍ صَدَقَةٌ وَكُلِّ تَحْمِيدَةٍ صَدَقَةٌ وَكُلِّ تَهْلِيلَةٍ صَدَقَةٌ وَأَمْرٌ بِالْمَعْرُوفِ صَدَقَةٌ وَنَهْىٌ عَنْ مُنْكَرٍ صَدَقَةٌ وَفِي بُضْعِ أَحَدِكُمْ صَدَقَةٌ " . قَالُوا يَا رَسُولَ اللَّهِ أَيَأْتِي أَحَدُنَا شَهْوَتَهُ وَيَكُونُ لَهُ فِيهَا أَجْرٌ قَالَ " أَرَأَيْتُمْ لَوْ وَضَعَهَا فِي حَرَامٍ أَكَانَ عَلَيْهِ فِيهَا وِزْرٌ فَكَذَلِكَ إِذَا وَضَعَهَا فِي الْحَلاَلِ كَانَ لَهُ أَجْرٌ "

"Abu Dharr reported: Some of the people from among the Companions of the Messenger of Allah (ﷺ) said to him: Messenger of Allah, the rich have taken away (all the) reward. They observe prayer as we do; they keep the fasts as we keep, and they give *Sadaqa* out of their surplus riches. Upon this he (the Holy Prophet) said: Has Allah not prescribed for you (a course) by following which you can (also) do *sadaqa*? In every declaration of the glorification of Allah (i. e. saying *Subhan Allah*) there is a *Sadaqa*, and every *Takbir* (i. e. saying Allah-O-

Akbar) is a *sadaqa*, and every praise of His (saying *alhamdu lillah*) is a *Sadaqa* and every declaration that He is One (*La illha ill-Allah*) is a *sadaqa*, and enjoining of good is a *sadaqa*, and forbidding of that which is evil is a *Sadaqa*, and in man's sexual intercourse (with his wife) there is a *Sadaqa*. They (the Companions) said: Messenger of Allah, is there reward for him who satisfies his sexual passion among us? He said: Tell me, if he were to devote it to something forbidden, would it not be a sin on his part? Similarly, if he were to devote it to something lawful, he should have a reward."

Spreading the bedroom secrets

Imam Muslim narrated in his *Saheeh* no. 1437 that Messenger of Allah (ﷺ) said:

إِنَّ مِنْ أَعْظَمِ الأَمَانَةِ عِنْدَ اللَّهِ يَوْمَ الْقِيَامَةِ الرَّجُلَ يُفْضِي إِلَى امْرَأَتِهِ وَتُفْضِي إِلَيْهِ ثُمَّ يَنْشُرُ سِرَّهَا

"The most important of the trusts in the sight of Allah on the Day of judgment is that a man goes to his wife and she goes to him (and the breach of this trust is) that he should divulge her secret."

Imam Ahmad narrated a sound *hadith* in his *Musnad* no. 27583:

حَدَّثَتْنِي أَسْمَاءُ بِنْتُ يَزِيدَ، أَنَّهَا كَانَتْ عِنْدَ رَسُولِ اللَّهِ صَلَّى اللهُ عَلَيْهِ وَسَلَّمَ وَالرِّجَالُ وَالنِّسَاءُ قُعُودٌ عِنْدَهُ فَقَالَ: " لَعَلَّ رَجُلًا يَقُولُ: مَا يَفْعَلُ بِأَهْلِهِ، وَلَعَلَّ امْرَأَةً تُخْبِرُ بِمَا فَعَلَتْ مَعَ زَوْجِهَا فَأَرَمَّ الْقَوْمُ " فَقُلْتُ: إِي وَاللَّهِ يَا رَسُولَ اللَّهِ، إِنَّهُنَّ لَيَقُلْنَ وَإِنَّهُمْ لَيَفْعَلُونَ قَالَ: «فَلَا تَفْعَلُوا فَإِنَّمَا مِثْلُ ذَلِكَ الشَّيْطَانُ لَقِيَ شَيْطَانَةً فِي طَرِيقٍ فَغَشِيَهَا وَالنَّاسُ يَنْظُرُونَ»

From Asma bint Yazid who narrated "that she was once in the presence of the Prophet (ﷺ) and there were both men and women sitting. The Prophet (ﷺ) then said: "Perhaps a man might discuss what he does with his wife, or perhaps a woman might inform someone what she did with her husband?"

The people were silent. Then I said: "O, Yes! O Messenger of Allah (ﷺ) .Verily both the women and men do that." Then the Prophet (ﷺ) said: "Do not do that. It is like a male satan who meets a female satan along the way, and has sex with her while the people look on!"

This is very common between the young and the old. Many people think it is entertaining that they sit with a group of friends or relatives and discuss their intimate relations. Many men even go to the extent of describing their wives and every detail that took place. From the adverse effects this has on the minds of those listening is that they will start imagining the situation and it might even sow jealousy, hatred and envy in the hearts of those who do not experience such things with their spouses. This also causes many marriages to break when one of the spouses, who dislike such secrets to be exposed, find out that their husband or wife have been spreading this secret which is supposed to be the most private matter between them. There have been many cases where one starts to harbor feelings for the spouse of another person because they do not receive such a thing from their own spouse and Allah is sought for aid. This is a very dangerous issue and causes many tribulations one cannot even imagine, which is why this is one of the worst things a person will come with in front of Allah.

The Blissful Union ©2017 Syed ISBN 978-93-5268-923-1

Obligation of wedding banquet (Walima)

Imam al-Bukhari narrated in his *Saheeh* no.5155

أَنَّ النَّبِيَّ صلى الله عليه وسلم رَأَى عَلَى عَبْدِ الرَّحْمَنِ بْنِ عَوْفٍ أَثَرَ صُفْرَةٍ قَالَ " مَا هَذَا ". قَالَ إِنِّي تَزَوَّجْتُ امْرَأَةً عَلَى وَزْنِ نَوَاةٍ مِنْ ذَهَبٍ. قَالَ " بَارَكَ اللَّهُ لَكَ، أَوْلِمْ وَلَوْ بِشَاةٍ ".

The Prophet (ﷺ) saw the traces of Sufra (yellow perfume) on `Abdur-Rahman bin Auf and said, "What is this?" `Abdur-Rahman, said, "I have married a woman and have paid gold equal to the weight of a datestone (as her *Mahr*). The Prophet (ﷺ) said to him, "May Allah bless you: Offer a wedding banquet even with one sheep."

Imam al-Bukhari narrated in his *Saheeh* no.5154

عَنْ أَنَسٍ، قَالَ أَوْلَمَ النَّبِيُّ صلى الله عليه وسلم بِزَيْنَبَ فَأَوْسَعَ الْمُسْلِمِينَ خَيْرًا فَخَرَجَ ـ كَمَا يَصْنَعُ إِذَا تَزَوَّجَ ـ فَأَتَى حُجَرَ أُمَّهَاتِ الْمُؤْمِنِينَ يَدْعُو وَيَدْعُونَ {لَهُ} ثُمَّ انْصَرَفَ فَرَأَى رَجُلَيْنِ فَرَجَعَ لاَ أَدْرِي آخْبَرْتُهُ أَوْ أُخْبِرَ بِخُرُوجِهِمَا.

Narrated Anas: The Prophet (ﷺ) offered a wedding banquet on the occasion of his marriage to Zainab, and provided a good meal for the Muslims. Then he went out as was his custom on marrying, he came to the dwelling places of the mothers of the Believers (i.e. his wives) invoking good (on them), and they were invoking good (on him). Then he departed (and came back) and saw two men (still sitting there). So he left again. I do not remember whether I informed him or he was informed (by somebody else) of their departure).

Accepting invitation of wedding feast

Imam Muslim narrated in his *Saheeh* no.1431 that Messenger of Allah (ﷺ) said:

" إِذَا دُعِيَ أَحَدُكُمْ فَلْيُجِبْ فَإِنْ كَانَ صَائِمًا فَلْيُصَلِّ وَإِنْ كَانَ مُفْطِرًا فَلْيَطْعَمْ ".

If any one of you is invited, he should accept (the invitation). In case he is fasting, he should pray (in order to bless the inmates of the house), and if he is not fasting he should eat.

Imam al-Bukhari narrated in his *Saheeh* no. 5173 that Messenger of Allah (ﷺ) said:

إِذَا دُعِيَ أَحَدُكُمْ إِلَى الْوَلِيمَةِ فَلْيَأْتِهَا

If anyone of you is invited to a wedding banquet, he must go for it (accept the invitation).

And he narrated in the next *hadith* of same chapter no.5174 that Messenger of Allah (ﷺ) said:

فُكُّوا الْعَانِيَ، وَأَجِيبُوا الدَّاعِيَ، وَعُودُوا الْمَرِيضَ

"Set the captives free, accept the invitation (to a wedding banquet), and visit the patients."

The Blissful Union ©2017 Syyed ISBN 978-93-5268-923-1

Inviting righteous people to the wedding banquet

Imam Abu Dawood reported in his *Sunan* no.4832 with an authentic chain that Messenger of Allah (ﷺ) said:

" لاَ تُصَاحِبْ إِلاَّ مُؤْمِنًا وَلاَ يَأْكُلْ طَعَامَكَ إِلاَّ تَقِيٌّ

Do not befriend but a believer and let only a righteous person eat your food.

This command from the Prophet (ﷺ) has great wisdom in it. The people that one invites most to their homes are the closest of their friends. If someone has an evil or a person of low character as their best or close friend he will enter his home and eat from his home the most. The Prophet (ﷺ) advised us to keep righteous people as our close friends and let only righteous people eat of our food as keeping righteous company helps one maintain his religion.

The Blissful Union ©2017 Syed ISBN 978-93-5268-923-1

Wedding banquet where poor are not invited

Imam al-Bukhari narrated in his *Saheeh* no.5177

عَنْ أَبِي هُرَيْرَةَ، رضى الله عنه أَنَّهُ كَانَ يَقُولُ شَرُّ الطَّعَامِ طَعَامُ الْوَلِيمَةِ يُدْعَى لَهَا الأَغْنِيَاءُ، وَيُتْرَكُ الْفُقَرَاءُ، وَمَنْ تَرَكَ الدَّعْوَةَ فَقَدْ عَصَى اللَّهَ وَرَسُولَهُ صلى الله عليه وسلم

Narrated Abu Huraira: The worst food is that of a wedding banquet to which only the rich are invited while the poor are not invited. And he who refuses an invitation (to a banquet) disobeys Allah and His Messenger (ﷺ).

Should a person return if he sees something objectionable in the party?

Imam al-Bukhari narrated in his *Saheeh* under the chapter

باب هَلْ يَرْجِعُ إِذَا رَأَى مُنْكَرًا فِي الدَّعْوَةِ

Chapter: Should a person return if he sees something objectionable in the party? no. 5181

عَنْ عَائِشَةَ، زَوْجِ النَّبِيِّ صلى الله عليه وسلم أَنَّهَا أَخْبَرَتْهُ أَنَّهَا اشْتَرَتْ نُمْرُقَةً فِيهَا تَصَاوِيرُ، فَلَمَّا رَآهَا رَسُولُ اللَّهِ صلى الله عليه وسلم قَامَ عَلَى الْبَابِ فَلَمْ يَدْخُلْ، فَعَرَفْتُ فِي وَجْهِهِ الْكَرَاهِيَةَ فَقُلْتُ يَا رَسُولَ اللَّهِ أَتُوبُ إِلَى اللَّهِ وَإِلَى رَسُولِهِ، مَاذَا أَذْنَبْتُ فَقَالَ رَسُولُ اللَّهِ صلى الله عليه وسلم " مَا بَالُ هَذِهِ النِّمْرِقَةِ ". قَالَتْ فَقُلْتُ اشْتَرَيْتُهَا لَكَ لِتَقْعُدَ عَلَيْهَا وَتَوَسَّدَهَا. فَقَالَ رَسُولُ اللَّهِ صلى الله عليه وسلم " إِنَّ أَصْحَابَ هَذِهِ الصُّوَرِ يُعَذَّبُونَ يَوْمَ الْقِيَامَةِ، وَيُقَالُ لَهُمْ أَحْيُوا مَا خَلَقْتُمْ ". وَقَالَ " إِنَّ الْبَيْتَ الَّذِي فِيهِ الصُّوَرُ لاَ تَدْخُلُهُ الْمَلاَئِكَةُ ".

Narrated Aisha: (the wife of the Prophet) I bought a cushion having on it pictures (of animals). When Allah's Messenger (ﷺ) saw it, he stood at the door and did not enter. I noticed the sign of disapproval on his face and said, "O Allah's Messenger (ﷺ)! I repent to Allah and His Apostle. What sin have I committed?' Allah's Messenger (ﷺ) said. "What is this cushion?" I said, "I have bought it for you so that you may sit on it and recline on it." Allah's Messenger (ﷺ) said, "The makers of these pictures will be punished on the Day of Resurrection, and it will be said to them, 'Give life to what you have created (i.e., these pictures).' " The Prophet (ﷺ) added,

"The Angels of (Mercy) do not enter a house in which there are pictures (of animals).

Photography and videography at the wedding party

Shaykh Muhammad bin Saalih al-Uthaymeen said: “In addition to the reservations about taking pictures at wedding parties as mentioned above, there is a very serious reservation which is: We have heard that some women bring cameras with them to take pictures of this celebration, and I do not know what justification these women have for taking pictures at these parties which are then spread among the people, intentionally or otherwise. Do those who take the pictures think that anyone approves of their actions? I do not think that anyone approves of what they do; I do not think that anyone would like his daughter’s or wife’s picture to be taken and kept by those misguided women to show to whomever they want, whenever they want? Would any of you agree for his *mahrams*’ pictures to be in the hands of other people, to be a source of mockery if they are ugly and a provocation of desire if they are beautiful?

We have even heard of something that is worse than that: that some people bring a video camera to these parties to take moving pictures, and they watch it themselves or show it to others every time they want to enjoy looking at these scenes.

We have also heard that some those who go to these parties and videotape them are young men, who mix with women at these parties or they sit alone with them, and no wise person who has any knowledge of the sources of *sharee’ah* will doubt

The Blissful Union ©2017 Syed ISBN 978-93-5268-923-1

that this is evil and is *haram*, and that it is stooping to the lowest level of imitating the *kuffar*."[14]

Another scenario that also occurs in today's time is where people spend extravagantly for such things and the *fitna* that is prevalent in many societies where male photographers are being invited to take pictures and videos of the bride, and many times these are sisters who wear hijab otherwise and are known to be religious, yet the day when they are beautified the most, a man is called to spend hours taking pictures and videos of her.

---

14 Friday Khutbah in the Jami' Mosque of 'Unayzah, entitled Munkaraat al-Afraah Mahaadhir Laylat al-Zafaaf taken from IslamQA website

Kissing while fasting

Imam Muslim narrated in his *Saheeh* no. 1106 under chapter

باب بَيَانِ أَنَّ الْقُبْلَةَ فِي الصَّوْمِ لَيْسَتْ مُحَرَّمَةً عَلَى مَنْ لَمْ تُحَرِّكْ شَهْوَتَهُ

Chapter: Clarifying that Kissing when fasting is not unlawful for the one whose desire is not provoked by that

عَنْ عَائِشَةَ، - رضى الله عنها - قَالَتْ كَانَ رَسُولُ اللَّهِ صلى الله عليه وسلم
يُقَبِّلُ إِحْدَى نِسَائِهِ وَهُوَ صَائِمٌ . ثُمَّ تَضْحَكُ

Aisha (Allah be pleased with her) said that the Messenger of Allah (ﷺ) kissed one of his wives while he was fasting, and then she (A'isha) laughed (as she narrated).

And in the same chapter its narrated

عَنْ عَائِشَةَ، - رضى الله عنها - قَالَتْ كَانَ رَسُولُ اللَّهِ صلى الله عليه وسلم
يُقَبِّلُ وَهُوَ صَائِمٌ وَيُبَاشِرُ وَهُوَ صَائِمٌ وَلَكِنَّهُ أَمْلَكُكُمْ لإِرْبِهِ

Aisha (Allah be pleased with her) reported: Allah's Messenger (ﷺ) used to kiss (his wives) while fasting and embraced (them) while fasting; but he had the greatest mastery over his desire among you.

Prohibition of having intercourse with wife during the day in Ramadan and expiation for that

Imam al-Bukhari narrated in his *Saheeh* no. 1936 under the chapter

بابُ إِذَا جَامَعَ فِي رَمَضَانَ وَلَمْ يَكُنْ لَهُ شَىْءٌ فَتُصُدِّقَ عَلَيْهِ فَلْيُكَفِّرْ

Chapter: Sexual intercourse with wife in Ramadan and the expiation of that.

أَنَّ أَبَا هُرَيْرَةَ ـ رضى الله عنه ـ قَالَ بَيْنَمَا نَحْنُ جُلُوسٌ عِنْدَ النَّبِيِّ صلى الله
عليه وسلم إِذْ جَاءَهُ رَجُلٌ، فَقَالَ يَا رَسُولَ اللَّهِ هَلَكْتُ. قَالَ " مَا لَكَ ". قَالَ وَقَعْتُ
عَلَى امْرَأَتِي وَأَنَا صَائِمٌ. فَقَالَ رَسُولُ اللَّهِ صلى الله عليه وسلم " هَلْ تَجِدُ رَقَبَةً
تُعْتِقُهَا ". قَالَ لاَ. قَالَ " فَهَلْ تَسْتَطِيعُ أَنْ تَصُومَ شَهْرَيْنِ مُتَتَابِعَيْنِ ". قَالَ لاَ.
فَقَالَ " فَهَلْ تَجِدُ إِطْعَامَ سِتِّينَ مِسْكِينًا ". قَالَ لاَ. قَالَ فَمَكَثَ النَّبِيُّ صلى الله
عليه وسلم، فَبَيْنَا نَحْنُ عَلَى ذَلِكَ أُتِيَ النَّبِيُّ صلى الله عليه وسلم بِعَرَقٍ فِيهَا
تَمْرٌ ـ وَالْعَرَقُ الْمِكْتَلُ ـ قَالَ " أَيْنَ السَّائِلُ ". فَقَالَ أَنَا. قَالَ " خُذْهَا فَتَصَدَّقْ بِهِ
". فَقَالَ الرَّجُلُ أَعَلَى أَفْقَرَ مِنِّي يَا رَسُولَ اللَّهِ فَوَاللَّهِ مَا بَيْنَ لاَبَتَيْهَا ـ يُرِيدُ
الْحَرَّتَيْنِ ـ أَهْلُ بَيْتٍ أَفْقَرُ مِنْ أَهْلِ بَيْتِي، فَضَحِكَ النَّبِيُّ صلى الله عليه وسلم
حَتَّى بَدَتْ أَنْيَابُهُ ثُمَّ قَالَ " أَطْعِمْهُ أَهْلَكَ "

Narrated Abu Huraira:

While we were sitting with the Prophet (ﷺ) a man came and said, "O Allah's Messenger (ﷺ)! I have been ruined." Allah's Messenger (ﷺ) asked what was the matter with him. He replied "I had sexual intercourse with my wife while I was fasting." Allah's Messenger (ﷺ) asked him, "Can you afford to manumit a slave?" He replied in the negative. Allah's Messenger (ﷺ) asked him, "Can you fast for two successive months?" He replied in the negative. The Prophet (ﷺ) asked him, "Can you afford to feed sixty poor persons?" He replied in the negative. The Prophet (ﷺ) kept silent and while we were in that state, a big basket full of dates was brought to the Prophet (ﷺ) . He asked, "Where is the questioner?" He replied, "I (am here)." The Prophet (ﷺ) said (to him), "Take this (basket of dates) and give it in charity." The man said, "Should I give it to a person poorer than I? By Allah; there is no family between its (i.e. Medina's) two mountains who are poorer than I." The Prophet (ﷺ) smiled till his premolar teeth became visible and then said, 'Feed your family with it."

The Blissful Union ©2017 Syed ISBN 978-93-5268-923-1

Intercourse during pregnancy

There is no difference of opinion among scholars that intercourse during pregnancy is allowed. Shaykh Ibn Uthaymeen said as its reported in *Fataawa al-Ulamaa fi Ushrat al-Nisaa* page 55:

يجوز للإنسان أن يُجامع زوجته الحامل متى شاء إلا إذا كان ذلك يضرّها ، فإنه يحرم عليه أن يفعل ما يضر بها ، وإن كان لا يضرها ولكن يشق عليها فإن الأولى عدم مجامعتها ، لأن اجتناب ما يشق عليها من حسن العشرة ، وقد قال تعالى : وعاشروهن بالمعروف

It is permissible for a man to have intercourse with his pregnant wife whenever he wishes, except if that will cause her harm, for it is *haram* for him to do anything that will cause her harm. If it will not cause her harm but it is difficult upon her, then it is better to avoid intercourse with her, because avoiding things which are difficult upon her is part of living with her with kind treatment towards her. Allah says: “and live with them honorably”

Doctors say that as long as your pregnancy is proceeding normally, you can have intercourse as often as you like.

Ruling on Pornography

Pornography in every form like movies, pictures, cartoons, plays etc is *haram* and sinful. Its a disease. And its not permissible for couple to watch pornography to stimulate themselves.
Allah says in Al-Quran (24:30):

قُل لِّلْمُؤْمِنِينَ يَغُضُّوا۟ مِنْ أَبْصَـٰرِهِمْ وَيَحْفَظُوا۟ فُرُوجَهُمْ ۚ ذَٰلِكَ أَزْكَىٰ لَهُمْ ۗ إِنَّ ٱللَّهَ
خَبِيرٌۢ بِمَا يَصْنَعُونَ

Tell the believing men to lower their gaze (from looking at forbidden things), and protect their private parts (from illegal sexual acts). That is purer for them. Verily, Allah is All-Aware of what they do.

Allah says in Al-Quran (24:31):

وَقُل لِّلْمُؤْمِنَـٰتِ يَغْضُضْنَ مِنْ أَبْصَـٰرِهِنَّ وَيَحْفَظْنَ فُرُوجَهُنَّ

And tell the believing women to lower their gaze (from looking at forbidden things), and protect their private parts (from illegal sexual acts)

Imam at-Tirmidhi reported in his *Jami at-Tirmidhi* no.2793 with an authentic chain that Messenger of Allah (ﷺ) said:

لاَ يَنْظُرُ الرَّجُلُ إِلَى عَوْرَةِ الرَّجُلِ وَلاَ تَنْظُرُ الْمَرْأَةُ إِلَى عَوْرَةِ الْمَرْأَةِ وَلاَ يُفْضِي الرَّجُلُ إِلَى الرَّجُلِ فِي الثَّوْبِ الْوَاحِدِ وَلاَ تُفْضِي الْمَرْأَةُ إِلَى الْمَرْأَةِ فِي الثَّوْبِ الْوَاحِدِ

A man is not to look at the '*Awrah* (private part) of a man, and a woman is not to look at the '*Awrah* (private part) of a woman. A man is not to be alone with a man under one garment, and a woman is not to be alone with a woman under one garment.

Scholars of permanent committee *(al-Lajnah al-Daa'imah)* presided by Shaykh Abdul Azeez bin Baaz, Fatwa no. 2424 gave verdict that its *haraam* by citing various evidences.

Advice To Those Who Are Tried of Watching Porn – Shaykh Abdur-Razzaq al-Badr (Teacher at Masjid An-Nabawi in Madeenah)

Questioner:

"May Allah reward you and may Allah bless you. May Allah benefit us with that which we have heard; and may Allah forgive us, you and all the Muslims.

This questioner, O' Shaykh, says: I implore you, by Allah, to ask this question (for me). He says in his question: "O' Shaykh, give me advice, for by Allah, I am upon the brink of the Hellfire.

For I have been addicted, O Shaykh, to pornography websites since last year. Every time I repent, I return to it again.

By Allah, the thing which I hate the most in these sites, but they overpower me every time and they are the reason for my failure. I used to be very successful in my work and in my studies, however, now I am in a state of loss."

Shaykh Abdur Razzaq al-Badr: "Firstly, I say, just as Umar ibn al-Khattaab, may Allah be pleased with him, has said: "Supplicate to Allah the Blessed and High that He turns the heart of your brother; that He guides him and accepts his repentance."

So we ask Allah the Mighty and Majestic, the Generous, Lord of the Great Throne, that He guides him and accepts his repentance; and that He makes us and him firm with the firm statement and that He gives us refuge from the evil of our souls and the evil of our actions.
I advise you, O' noble brother, with one piece of advice; always be mindful of it, for in it is salvation for you. It is the greatest admonition. Always bear in mind that Allah, the Lord of all that exists, sees you and that He, Glorified and Exalted be He, is looking at you. If you are alone within the house on any day, then do not say: "I am alone," but say: "There is a *Raqeeb* (Watcher i.e Allah) over me.

When you sit, in this seclusion with this screen on the internet and you begin to enter those sites and you think that no one from the people can see you, then know that the Lord of all that exists is looking at you.

"Knows he not that Allah does see (what he does)?" Al-Quran (96:14)

In this verse is a rebuke for you; treat yourself with it; rebuke yourself by way of the Qur'an.

There is no harm if you put this verse upon your room in front of you so that you can look at it and it can deter you and rebuke you from that matter, which there is not to be seen nor will you find therein any result that will benefit you. Rather, you have been affected in your studies, in your manners, in your worship, in your performance; there is no beneficial fruit in it.

This is what the enemies of the religion desire; when they make the likes of these despicable, licentious, and harmful films;

So that the children of the Muslims become lost, and the children of the Muslims become like cattle. Rather, they are even more astray; in following of desires and urges, deviations and misguidances. Due to this, have *Taqwa* of Allah the Mighty and Majestic, and make yourself constant in turning to Allah the Glorified and High, and in sincere *Tawbah* to Allah the Mighty and Majestic.

This device, I do not say to you, to utilize it for permissible affairs; rather, I say: remove it from the house completely. Remove it from the house completely, and it should not remain with you even for a second. Tonight, remove it from your house, because its presence is an apparent corruption for you. It should not remain with you in hopes of benefitting from it in useful ways. Rather, remove it from your house completely and close off this door of evil from yourself and turn to Allah the Glorified and High.

We ask Allah to turn your heart and to accept your repentance, and to accept all of our repentance, and to guide us all to the (straight) path, and to rectify for us all of our affairs, indeed He, Blessed and Exalted be He, is the All-Hearing, Ever-Responsive, and Ever-Near."[15]

---

[15] Video available at the website of DuSunnah Translated by: Raha ibn Donald Batts

Effects of pornography on marriage

The effects of porn on marriage are devastating. It is a major threat to marriages, the family, and the society at large. Here are some adverse effects of pornography on marriage.

1) Men who are addicted to pornography will be unable to be satisfied with their wives, causing marital problems or even divorce.

2) Research by Michael Malcolm and George S published in *Eastern Economic Journal* in 2016 shows that people who watch porn have decreased libido when it comes to making love to their spouse. The spouse is not what turns them on.

3) Watching porn decreases sexual pleasure. According to study by Dolf Zillmann and Jennings Bryant titled *"Pornography's Impact on Sexual Satisfaction"* published in the *Journal of Applied social psychology* 'watching porn decreases sexual pleasure'.

4) It makes real sex and even the real world boring in comparison. Regular intercourse is not depicted in porn, so the person who watches porn starts to get a warped view of what sex really is.

The Blissful Union ©2017 Syed ISBN 978-93-5268-923-1

5) It creates comparisons. You can't look at images without comparing those images to your spouse. This can lead to ungratefulness, where a person focuses on what is absent in his/her spouse instead of being thankful for what he/she is. The "fantasy women" in pornography are portrayed as unrealistically sexually attractive, often because of plastic surgery, stage makeup and digital editing. It is impossible for a real woman to match up to these fantasy women.
6) It destroys self-esteem in women, since its impossible for a real woman to match up to these fantasy women,this will make her feel inferior and insecure as research published in *The Journal of Men's Studies* in 2006 suggests.

7) It breaks trust. When women discover that their husbands have been viewing pornography they experience a variety of emotions: anger, hurt, sadness, betrayal, and rejection. And for modest women this is a violation of marital trust.

8) Pornography leads to perversity. Due to its inability to satisfy, pornography always leads one to greater perversity as established in research published by *Journal of Family Violence* in 2009.

9) It creates unreal expectations. It depicts unrealistic sexual scenarios which is not practical in real life.

Spending time with your spouse

Married couples often complain about losing the spark in their relationship after a few years into their marriage. This is because they start taking each other for granted and no longer do special things that they used to. Spending quality time together is very important to keep your marriage strong. Your spouse should be your best friend and you should enjoy spending time with them most. Spending time with your spouse alone, where it's just the two of you, is an essential part of marriage. Try looking for something both of you enjoy. It would be even more romantic if you would take your time out to do something your spouse loves to just show them how much you care for them.

And the best example is what we have in our Messenger (ﷺ)

Imam Al-Bukhari narrtaed in his *Saheeh* no. 5236

عنْ عَائِشَةَ ـ رضى الله عنها ـ قَالَتْ رَأَيْتُ النَّبِيَّ صلى الله عليه وسلم يَسْتُرُنِي بِرِدَائِهِ، وَأَنَا أَنْظُرُ إِلَى الْحَبَشَةِ يَلْعَبُونَ فِي الْمَسْجِدِ، حَتَّى أَكُونَ أَنَا الَّذِي أَسْأَمُ، فَاقْدُرُوا قَدْرَ الْجَارِيَةِ الْحَدِيثَةِ السِّنِّ الْحَرِيصَةِ عَلَى اللَّهْوِ.

Narrated Aisha: The Prophet (ﷺ) was screening me with his *Rida* (garment covering the upper part of the body) while I was looking at the Ethiopians who were playing in the courtyard of the mosque. (I continued watching) till I was satisfied. So you may deduce from this event how a little girl (who has not reached the age of puberty) who is eager to enjoy amusement should be treated in this respect.

Playing sport with your spouse

According to research published in 2000 in *the Journal of Personality and Social Psychology* by psychologist Arthur Aron: the couple that plays together stays together. Also taking part in sports with your significant other can improve your relationship off the playing field. Not only will you bond over a shared activity or learn something new, you will stay fit.

Marriage is supposed to be fun! If you have fallen into a boring habit and forgotten that, then it's time to try something new and rekindle your spirit of sport. You can try racing with your spouse, wrestling, having water fight, badminton, tennis and so on.

Imam Abu Dawood narrated in his *Sunan* no. 2578 with an authentic chain

عَنْ عَائِشَةَ، رَضِيَ اللَّهُ عَنْهَا أَنَّهَا كَانَتْ مَعَ النَّبِيِّ صلى الله عليه وسلم فِي سَفَرٍ قَالَتْ فَسَابَقْتُهُ فَسَبَقْتُهُ عَلَى رِجْلَىَّ فَلَمَّا حَمَلْتُ اللَّحْمَ سَابَقْتُهُ فَسَبَقَنِي فَقَالَ " هَذِهِ بِتِلْكَ السَّبْقَةِ " .

Narrated Aisha while she was on a journey along with the Messenger of Allah (ﷺ): I had a race with him (the Prophet) and I outstripped him on my feet. When I became fleshy, (again) I had a race with him (the Prophet) and he outstripped me. He said: This is for that outstripping.

Imam Ahmad narrated this authentic *hadith* with extra wording in his *Musnad* no.26277

عَنْ عَائِشَةَ، قَالَتْ: خَرَجْتُ مَعَ النَّبِيِّ صَلَّى اللهُ عَلَيْهِ وَسَلَّمَ فِي بَعْضِ أَسْفَارِهِ
وَأَنَا جَارِيَةٌ لَمْ أَحْمِلِ اللَّحْمَ وَلَمْ أَبْدُنْ، فَقَالَ لِلنَّاسِ: «تَقَدَّمُوا» فَتَقَدَّمُوا، ثُمَّ قَالَ
لِي: «تَعَالَيْ حَتَّى أُسَابِقَكِ» فَسَابَقْتُهُ فَسَبَقْتُهُ، فَسَكَتَ عَنِّي، حَتَّى إِذَا حَمَلْتُ
اللَّحْمَ وَبَدُنْتُ وَنَسِيتُ، خَرَجْتُ مَعَهُ فِي بَعْضِ أَسْفَارِهِ، فَقَالَ لِلنَّاسِ: «تَقَدَّمُوا»
فَتَقَدَّمُوا، ثُمَّ قَالَ: «تَعَالَيْ حَتَّى أُسَابِقَكِ» فَسَابَقْتُهُ، فَسَبَقَنِي، فَجَعَلَ يَضْحَكُ،
وَهُوَ يَقُولُ: «هَذِهِ بِتِلْكَ»

Aisha said: Once I traveled with Allah's Messenger (ﷺ) when I was young and not fat. Then, he asked his companions to go forward and they did so. Afterwards he said, Let us race each other. Therefore, I started to run until I won. Later on when I became fat and forgot what had happened, I traveled again with him. He asked his companions to go forward and they did so. Then he said, Let us race each other. I forgot what happened in the first race. I was fat therefore I said, O messenger of Allah (ﷺ) , how could I race you in this case? However, he said, Let us race. Then, he won the race. He started to laugh and said, This one is for the last one.

Treating your wife kindly

Allah says in Al-Quran (4:19):

وَعَاشِرُوهُنَّ بِٱلۡمَعۡرُوفِۚ

And live with them honourably

Its reported in *Jami at-Tirmidhi* no. 1162 with an authentic chain that Messenger of Allah (ﷺ) said:

كْمَلُ الْمُؤْمِنِينَ إِيمَانًا أَحْسَنُهُمْ خُلُقًا وَخِيَارُكُمْ خِيَارُكُمْ لِنِسَائِهِمْ خُلُقًا

"The most complete of the believers in faith, is the one with the best character among them. And the best of you are those who are best to your women."

Being nice includes good communication. A husband should be willing to open up, and be willing to listen to his wife. He should not forget to ask her about what irritates her.

The Blissful Union ©2017 Syed ISBN 978-93-5268-923-1

Dealing with wife whom you dislike

If this question were to be asked to people today that how would their dealings be with their wife if they disliked her, the most common answer would be that they would divorce her. This is a dilemma that has affected the muslim nation. People resort to divorce even for the most petty issues. Statistics state that the divorce rate in the muslim lands has increased. Every year the rate of divorce becomes higher for reasons which can be resolved in their homes, yet they resort to divorce.
It is natural that one will dislike few characteristics in their spouse because human is created with imperfections and shortcomings but that does not necessarily mean they will need to get a divorce.

Allah says in Al-Quran (4:19)

وَعَاشِرُوهُنَّ بِٱلْمَعْرُوفِ فَإِن كَرِهْتُمُوهُنَّ فَعَسَىٰٓ أَن تَكْرَهُوا۟ شَيْـًٔا وَيَجْعَلَ ٱللَّهُ فِيهِ خَيْرًا كَثِيرًا

And live with them honorably. If you dislike them, it may be that you dislike a thing and Allah brings through it a great deal of good.

Imam Ibn Kathir commented on this Ayah in his *Tafseer* (2/212) stating:

أَيْ فَعَسَى أَنْ يَكُونَ صَبْرُكُمْ مَعَ إِمْسَاكِكُمْ لَهُنَّ وَكَرَاهَتِهِنَّ فِيهِ، خَيْرٌ كَثِيرٌ لَكُمْ فِي الدُّنْيَا وَالْآخِرَةِ، كَمَا قَالَ ابْنُ عَبَّاسٍ فِي هَذِهِ الْآيَةِ: هُوَ أَنْ يَعْطِفَ عَلَيْهَا فَيُرْزَقَ مِنْهَا وَلَدًا، وَيَكُونُ فِي ذَلِكَ الْوَلَدِ خَيْرٌ كَثِيرٌ

Allah says that your patience, which is demonstrated by keeping wives whom you dislike, carries good rewards for you in this life and the Hereafter. Ibn Abbas commented on this Ayah, "That the husband may feel compassion towards his wife and Allah gives him a child with her, and this child carries tremendous goodness."

Messenger of Allah (ﷺ) said in *hadith* reported by Imam Muslim in his *Saheeh* no.1468:

لاَ يَفْرَكْ مُؤْمِنٌ مُؤْمِنَةً إِنْ كَرِهَ مِنْهَا خُلُقًا رَضِيَ مِنْهَا آخَرَ

"A believing man should not hate a believing woman; if he dislikes one of her characteristics, he will be pleased with another."

Along with the characteristics that a man or woman will dislike in their spouse there will also be many other characteristics that they will love about their other half. It is upon us to concentrate and emphasize on the good characteristics and overlook the bad ones. This will help couples keep the love blooming and the relationship strong. It is upon both that they try their level best to keep the marriage going unless they come to the conclusion, after having tried everything prescribed in the *shareeah*, that separation will be the best solution for both spouses.

Imam Ibn Al Jawzi narrated an incident in his book *Sayd al-Khatir* no.1329:

" A man complained to me of his extreme dislike towards his wife and said: I cannot choose separation from her for a few reasons, from them are: Her numerous favors upon me, my lack of patience and I cannot safeguard my tongue from complaining. And in my speech she comes to know of my dislike towards her.
So I said to him: This (behaviour towards her) is not beneficial, Infact the houses are entered upon from their main doors (meaning you should be direct and not beat around the bush). It is upon you to seclude yourself and ponder, then you will realize that in reality it is the burden of your sins (which is why you harbor dislike for your wife), so increase in your repentance and asking forgiveness (from Allah).
As for showing her your dislike for her and hurting her, this is not going to benefit, as it was said by Al-Hasan bin Al-Hajjaj: It is a punishment of Allah upon you, so do not confront His punishment with the sword, but confront it with repentance.

And know that you are in a position of one who is being tested and you will be rewarded if you are patient upon it, (and you may dislike a thing while it is good for you) Al-Quran (2:216)!
So be patient with what Allah has decreed, and ask Him for relief (from trial), because if you combine between asking forgiveness and repentance from sins and between patience over the decree and asking for relief, it results in three types of worship (*Ibadah*) , you will be rewarded for each of these. And do not waste your time over things that will not benefit you, and do not think that you will be able to avert what is decreed, (And if Allah touches you with harm, none can remove it but He..) Al-Quran (6:17)"

And it is narrated in the same book by Imam Ibn Al Jawzi no. 1330 about this man:

“The man said: And this woman extremely loves me, and she excessively serves me, but still her hatred has become an instilled part of my nature.
I said to him: So be patient with her because it is from the decree of Allah, and you will be rewarded for it.
And it was to Abu Uthman An-Neesaboori: What is the action you have hope in the most (that you will have a goodly reward for it with Allah)? He said: In my youth, my family were forcing me to get married, and I rejected, then a woman came to me and said: O Abu Uthman! I desire you (for marriage), and I ask you by Allah to marry me, so she brought her father, he was poor, so he got her married to me and he was very happy about it. When she entered upon me (in seclusion), I saw that she was squint eyed, lame, deformed and ugly (face). But her love for me prevented me from leaving her, so I stayed (with her) in order not to break her heart and I never showed my dislike for her. It was as if I was on an unbearable hot piece of coal due to my (extreme) dislike for her, so I stayed like this for fifteen years until she passed away. So there is no action of mine that I have more hope in (as action that will please Allah) than this action of keeping her heart.

So I (Ibn Al Jawzi) said to him: This is what real men do! Is it more beneficial to the one undergoing this test that he makes his hatred apparent by hurting her? Rather, the way to deal with it is what I have mentioned to you, by repentance, patience and asking Allah to give you relief.

Shaykh Ibn Uthaymeen (may Allah have mercy on him) said:

What both spouses must do is to fulfill the duties enjoined by Allah of kind treatment, and the husband should not mistreat the wife because of his being of a higher status than her and being in charge of her affairs. Similarly it is not permissible for the wife to try to prove she is better than the husband. Rather both of them must treat the other kindly. It is well known that the husband may dislike the wife, either because she falls short in her duties towards him or because of some lack of intelligence and wisdom, and so on. How should he deal with this woman? We say: This is mentioned in the Qur'an and in the Sunnah. Allah, may He be blessed and exalted, says: "If you dislike them, it may be that you dislike a thing and Allah brings through it a great deal of good" Al-Quran (4:19)

And this happens in fact. A man may dislike his wife for some reason, but he shows patience, and Allah creates a lot of good in this, and the dislike turns to love, the lack of interest to delight, and so on .

And the Prophet (peace and blessings of Allah be upon him) said: "No believing man should hate a believing woman; if he dislikes one of her characteristics he will be pleased with another."

Look at this balanced view. Allah gave great wisdom to the Messenger (peace and blessings of Allah be upon him): "If he dislikes one of her characteristics he will be pleased with another." Does anyone get everything he wants in this world? No, not at all. You will never get everything you want in this world, and even if one thing is perfect, something else will be lacking, even days. Allah says (interpretation of the meaning): "And so are the days (good and not so good), that We give to men by turns" (Al-Quran 3:140) .Concerning that the *Jaahili* poet said: A day against us and a day for us, a day when we are sad and a day when we are happy.

Try this and you will find that it is true. The world does not stay the same. A well known saying is: It is impossible for

The Blissful Union ©2017 Syed ISBN 978-93-5268-923-1

things to stay the same. So if you dislike something about your wife, think instead of what you are pleased with, until you are convinced. [16]

Take care of women! A command from Messenger of Allah (ﷺ)

Imam Al-Bukhari narrated in his *Saheeh* no.3331 that Messenger of Allah (ﷺ) said:

اسْتَوْصُوا بِالنِّسَاءِ، فَإِنَّ الْمَرْأَةَ خُلِقَتْ مِنْ ضِلَعٍ، وَإِنَّ أَعْوَجَ شَيْءٍ فِي الضِّلَعِ
أَعْلاَهُ، فَإِنْ ذَهَبْتَ تُقِيمُهُ كَسَرْتَهُ، وَإِنْ تَرَكْتَهُ لَمْ يَزَلْ أَعْوَجَ، فَاسْتَوْصُوا بِالنِّسَاءِ

"Treat women nicely, for women is created from a rib, and the most curved portion of the rib is its upper portion, so, if you should try to straighten it, it will break, but if you leave it as it is, it will remain crooked. So treat women nicely."

Shaykh Ibn Uthaymeen explained this *hadith* in detail his *Sharh Riyadh as-Saliheen* (3/117-18), here is a summarization of what he said:

"Allah created Adam عليه السلام without a father or mother, but He created him from dust and then said to him Be and he was (created). And then Allah created from him his wife, so He created her from the bent part of his rib, it will remain bent. Even if you enjoy it, it will still have imperfection. And if you try to straighten it, you will break it. Similar is the case of the women. If man enjoys her, he will enjoy her along with this imperfection. A man will never find in any woman exactly how he wants her to be. She will definitely have shortcomings

---

[16] Liqaa'aat al-Baab il-Maftooh (introduction to part 159) taken from website IslamQA

and faults and that is natural. If he tries to straighten her he will never be able to do so, instead he will break her, and breaking her means separation from her (divorce).
In this is a counsel from the Prophet (ﷺ) for men to be kind towards their family and to deal with them in a good manner. And it is upon him to forgive as much as he can as in the saying of Allah: (Show forgiveness), meaning hold to forgiveness what is easy for him to forgive from the traits of people.
Man will not be able to find a woman who is free from fault or 100% the same as he desires and expects. But do as instructed by the Prophet (ﷺ), enjoy them ignoring this trait. Also, along with a characteristic you dislike about her, you will find a characteristic in her that you are pleased with. So deal with this in patience."

Men should understand that women are created differently than men, as stated in the *hadith* by our beloved Messenger (ﷺ), that women are created from the bent rib and the most crooked is the top portion. So, by nature, women will have some shortcomings and crookedness in their character. This *hadith* in no way is a green signal for women that they can mistreat their husbands, but it is a lesson for men, that no matter how much he tries to correct or straighten some traits, he will fail. Rather what can work better for both is that he treat her with love and compassion and overlook some of her traits. Taking care of her and treating her well can bear very sweet fruits in one's marital life.

Forbearing one's wife

Many men, by nature, have more ego than women do. When it comes to their wife questioning them about some matters, or giving them an opinion regarding anything, they feel that she has hurt his ego. This should not be the case. Rather, it is upon men to tolerate and forbear their wife's shortcomings especially regarding her tongue just as it is upon her to respect her husband's feelings. The greatest of mankind, our beloved messenger (ﷺ), used to tolerate some shortcomings from his wives, though they were the best of women. He would deal with them with patience and forbearance. In him we have the best example.

Imam Al-Bukhari narrated in his *Saheeh* no. 4913:

Narrated Ibn Abbas: For the whole year I had the desire to ask Umar bin Al-Khattab regarding the explanation of a Verse (in Surat Al-Tahrim) but I could not ask him because I respected him very much. When he went to perform the Hajj, I too went along with him. On our return, while we were still on the way home. `Umar went aside to answer the call of nature by the Arak trees. I waited till he finished and then I proceeded with him and asked him. "O chief of the Believers! Who were the two wives of the Prophet (ﷺ) who aided one another against him?" He said, "They were Hafsa and Aisha." Then I said to him, "By Allah, I wanted to ask you about this a year ago, but I could not do so owing to my respect for you." `Umar said,

"Do not refrain from asking me. If you think that I have knowledge (about a certain matter), ask me; and if I know (something about it), I will tell you." Then Umar added, "By Allah, in the pre-Islamic Period of Ignorance we did not pay attention to women until Allah revealed regarding them what He revealed regarding them and assigned for them what He has assigned. Once while I was thinking over a certain matter, my wife said, "I recommend that you do so-and-so." I said to her, "What have you got to do with the is matter? Why do you poke your nose in a matter which I want to see fulfilled.?" She said, How strange you are, O son of Al-Khattab! You don't want to be argued with whereas your daughter, Hafsa surely, argues with Allah's Messenger (ﷺ) so much that he remains angry for a full day!" `Umar then reported; how he at once put on his outer garment and went to Hafsa and said to her, "O my daughter! Do you argue with Allah's Messenger (ﷺ) so that he remains angry the whole day?" Hafsa said, "By Allah, we argue with him." `Umar said, "Know that I warn you of Allah's punishment and the anger of Allah's Messenger (ﷺ) . . . O my daughter! Don't be betrayed by the one who is proud of her beauty because of the love of Allah's Messenger (ﷺ) for her (i.e. Aisha)." Umar addled, "Then I went out to Um Salama's house who was one of my relatives, and I talked to her. She said, O son of Al-Khattab! It is rather astonishing that you interfere in everything; you even want to interfere between Allah's Apostle and his wives!' By Allah, by her talk she influenced me so much that I lost some of my anger. I left her (and went home). At that time I had a friend from the Ansar who used to bring news (from the Prophet) in case of my absence, and I used to bring him the news if he was absent. In those days we were afraid of one of the kings of Ghassan tribe. We heard that he intended to move and attack us, so fear filled our hearts because of that. (One day) my

The Blissful Union ©2017 Syed ISBN 978-93-5268-923-1

Ansari friend unexpectedly knocked at my door, and said, "Open Open!' I said, 'Has the king of Ghassan come? He said, 'No, but something worse; Allah's Messenger (ﷺ) has isolated himself from his wives.' I said, 'Let the nose of `Aisha and Hafsa be stuck to dust (i.e. humiliated)!' Then I put on my clothes and went to Allah's Messenger (ﷺ)'s residence, and behold, he was staying in an upper room of his to which he ascended by a ladder, and a black slave of Allah's Messenger (ﷺ) was (sitting) on the first step. I said to him, 'Say (to the Prophet (ﷺ)) Umar bin Al-Khattab is here.' Then the Prophet (ﷺ) admitted me and I narrated the story to Allah's Messenger (ﷺ). When I reached the story of Um Salama, Allah's Messenger (ﷺ) smiled while he was lying on a mat made of palm tree leaves with nothing between him and the mat. Underneath his head there was a leather pillow stuffed with palm fibres, and leaves of a saut tree were piled at his feet, and above his head hung a few water skins. On seeing the marks of the mat imprinted on his side, I wept. He said. 'Why are you weeping?' I replied, "O Allah's Messenger (ﷺ)! Caesar and Khosrau are leading the life (i.e. Luxurious life) while you, Allah's Messenger (ﷺ) though you are, is living in destitute". The Prophet (ﷺ) then replied. 'Won't you be satisfied that they enjoy this world and we the Hereafter?'

Man lying to his wife or a woman lying to her husband to strengthen ties of love between them

Imam Muslim narrated in his *Saheeh* no. 2605 that Messenger of Allah (ﷺ) said:

" لَيْسَ الْكَذَّابُ الَّذِي يُصْلِحُ بَيْنَ النَّاسِ وَيَقُولُ خَيْرًا وَيَنْمِي خَيْرًا " . قَالَ ابْنُ شِهَابٍ وَلَمْ أَسْمَعْ يُرَخَّصُ فِي شَىْءٍ مِمَّا يَقُولُ النَّاسُ كَذِبٌ إِلاَّ فِي ثَلاَثٍ الْحَرْبُ وَالإِصْلاَحُ بَيْنَ النَّاسِ وَحَدِيثُ الرَّجُلِ امْرَأَتَهُ وَحَدِيثُ الْمَرْأَةِ زَوْجَهَا

A liar is not one who tries to bring reconciliation amongst people and speaks good (in order to avert dispute), or he conveys good. Ibn Shihab said he did not hear that exemption was granted in anything what the people speak as lie but in three cases: in battle, for bringing reconciliation amongst persons and the narration of the words of the husband to his wife, and the narration of the words of a wife to her husband (in a twisted form in order to bring reconciliation between them).

Imam Tirmidhi narrated in his Jami at-Tirmidhi no.1939 with an authentic chain that Messenger of Allah (ﷺ) said:

لاَ يَحِلُّ الْكَذِبُ إِلاَّ فِي ثَلاَثٍ يُحَدِّثُ الرَّجُلُ امْرَأَتَهُ لِيُرْضِيَهَا وَالْكَذِبُ فِي الْحَرْبِ وَالْكَذِبُ لِيُصْلِحَ بَيْنَ النَّاسِ

It is not lawful to lie except in three cases: Something the man tells his wife to please her, to lie during war, and to lie in order to bring peace between the people.

Hafidh Ibn Hajr said in Fath Al-Bari (5/300) in explanation of this hadith:

وَاتَّفَقُوا عَلَى أَنَّ الْمُرَاد بِالْكَذِبِ فِي حَقّ الْمَرْأَة وَالرَّجُل إِنَّمَا هُوَ فِيمَا لَا يُسْقِط حَقًّا عَلَيْهِ أَوْ عَلَيْهَا أَوْ أَخْذ مَا لَيْسَ لَهُ أَوْ لَهَا

Its agreed upon that the meaning of husband lying to his wife and vice versa should not lead to violating rights of husband by the wife or the violation of rights of the wife, and (it should not lead him) to take what it not his or (that) she should not take what does not belong to her.

Shaykh Ibn Uthaymeen explained this in his *Sharh Riyad as-Saliheen* (1/1790):

"كذلك من المصلحة : حديث الرجل زوجته ، وحديث المرأة زوجها فيما يوجب الألفة والمودّة ، مثل أن يقول لها : أنت عندي غالية ، وأنت أحبّ إليّ من سائر النساء ، وما أشبه ذلك ، وإن كان كاذبًا ، لكن من أجل إلقاء المودّة ، والمصلحة تقتضي هذا "

From the beneficial matters is the speech of the husband towards his wife and the speech of the wife towards the husband be such that it creates love and affection, for example he says to her: you are very precious to me, and you are more beloved to me than all the women in this world, and the likes of such (statements), even if he is lying, but it should be with the intention of causing affection, and this is required for the purpose of benefit (i.e. to increase love in marriage).

Ghairah (protective jealousy)

Ghairah is to have protective jealousy towards one's spouse and it is an act that is praiseworthy in the sight of Allah. A man should have a sense of honor when it comes to his wife interacting or dealing with men who are impermissible for her to mix with and he should stop her where he sees that his wife might stray. And similarly, the wife should feel a sense of protectiveness and jealousy when it comes to her husband dealing with the opposite gender. This should be done in a manner that is balanced and one should not cross the limits set by *Sharee'ah* such that it should not lead one to become suspicious about their spouse which is a sin that leads to other sins like spying etc. Having *ghairah* protects both spouses from falling into sins as both of them will stop each other from committing that which is impermissible.

The man who does not show any concern towards his wife while she mixes freely with men who are impermissible for her and he does not stop her because he does not feel *ghairah* towards her is called a *'dayyooth'* as stated in a *hadith* of Messenger of Allah (ﷺ).

Imam An-Nasa'ee narrated in his *Sunan* no. 2562 with an authentic chain that the Messenger of Allah (ﷺ) said:

ثَلاَثَةٌ لاَ يَنْظُرُ اللهُ عَزَّ وَجَلَّ إِلَيْهِمْ يَوْمَ الْقِيَامَةِ الْعَاقُّ لِوَالِدَيْهِ وَالْمَرْأَةُ الْمُتَرَجِّلَةُ

The Blissful Union ©2017 Syed ISBN 978-93-5268-923-1

وَالدَّيُّوثُ

"There are three at whom Allah will not look on the Day of Resurrection: The one who disobeys his parents, the woman who imitates men in her outward appearance, and the *dayyooth*
.

Imam Al-Bukhari narrated in his *Saheeh* no. 5224:
"Narrated Asma' bint Abu Bakr: When Az-Zubair married me, he had no real property or any slave or anything else except a camel which drew water from the well, and his horse. I used to feed his horse with fodder and drew water and sew the bucket for drawing it, and prepare the dough, but I did not know how to bake bread. So our Ansari neighbors used to bake bread for me, and they were honorable ladies. I used to carry the date stones on my head from Zubair's land given to him by Allah's Messenger (ﷺ) and this land was two third *Farsakh* (about three miles) from my house. One day, while I was coming with the date stones on my head, I met Allah's Messenger (ﷺ) along with some Ansari people. He called me and then, (directing his camel to kneel down) said, "Ikh! Ikh!" so as to make me ride behind him (on his camel). I felt shy to travel with the men and remembered Az-Zubair and his sense of *Ghairah*, as he was one of those people who had the greatest sense of *Ghairah*. Allah's Messenger (ﷺ) noticed that I felt shy, so he proceeded. I came to Az-Zubair and said, "I met Allah's Messenger (ﷺ) while I was carrying a load of date stones on my head, and he had some companions with him. He made his camel kneel down so that I might ride, but I felt shy in his presence and remembered your sense of *Ghairah* (See the glossary). On that Az-Zubair said, "By Allah, your carrying the date stones (and you being seen by the Prophet (ﷺ) in such a state) is more shameful to me than your riding with him." (I continued serving in this way) till Abu Bakr sent me a

servant to look after the horse, whereupon I felt as if he had set me free."

It is reported in *Saheeh Al-Bukhari* no. 6846:

عَنِ الْمُغِيرَةِ، قَالَ قَالَ سَعْدُ بْنُ عُبَادَةَ لَوْ رَأَيْتُ رَجُلاً مَعَ امْرَأَتِي لَضَرَبْتُهُ
بِالسَّيْفِ غَيْرَ مُصْفَحٍ. فَبَلَغَ ذَلِكَ النَّبِيَّ صلى الله عليه وسلم فَقَالَ "
أَتَعْجَبُونَ مِنْ غَيْرَةِ سَعْدٍ، لأَنَا أَغْيَرُ مِنْهُ، وَاللَّهُ أَغْيَرُ مِنِّي "

Narrated Al-Mughira: Sa'd bin Ubada said, "If I found a man with my wife, I would kill him with the sharp side of my sword." When the Prophet (ﷺ) heard that he said, "Do you wonder at Sa'd's sense of *ghairah* (self-respect)? Verily, I have more sense of *ghairah* than Sa`d, and Allah has more sense of *ghairah* than I."

Using beautiful nicknames to address your wife

Imam Al-Bukhari narrated in his *Saheeh* no. 3768:

إنَّ عَائِشَةَ ـ رضى الله عنها ـ قَالَتْ قَالَ رَسُولُ اللَّهِ صلى الله عليه وسلم يَوْمًا " يَا عَائِشَ، هَذَا جِبْرِيلُ يُقْرِئُكِ السَّلاَمَ ". فَقُلْتُ وَعَلَيْهِ السَّلاَمُ وَرَحْمَةُ اللَّهِ وَبَرَكَاتُهُ، تَرَى مَا لاَ أَرَى. تُرِيدُ رَسُولَ اللَّهِ صلى الله عليه وسلم.

Aisha said, "Once Allah's Messenger (ﷺ) said (to me), 'O Aish! This is Gabriel greeting you. I said, 'Peace and Allah's Mercy and Blessings be on him, you see what I don't see' " She was addressing Allah 's Apostle.

In an authentic hadith reported by Imam An-Nasaee in his *Sunan Al-Kubra* no. 8902 : Messenger of Allah (ﷺ) addressed his wife Aisha (may Allah be pleased with her) as Humayra (little reddish).

فقال لي النبي صلى الله عليه وسلم: يا حميراء أتحبين أن تنظري إليهم.
فقلت: نعم

Prophet (ﷺ) told me: "O Humayra' (little reddish), do you like to watch them?" I (Aisha) said: Yes.

Using perfume for your spouse

Imam Abu Dawood reported in his *Sunan* no.4162 with an authentic chain:

عَنْ أَنَسِ بْنِ مَالِكٍ، قَالَ كَانَتْ لِلنَّبِيِّ صلى الله عليه وسلم سُكَّةٌ يَتَطَيَّبُ مِنْهَا

Narrated Anas ibn Malik: The Prophet (ﷺ) had *sikkah* with which he perfumed himself

Scent is one of the most under-appreciated aspects of attraction. According to research by M. Luisa Demattè and team entitled *'Olfactory Cues Modulate Facial Attractiveness"* published in *Oxford Journal of chemical senses* "scent also affects how people perceive us on an unconscious level".

Drinking from same place

Imam Muslim narrated in his *Saheeh* no.300:

عَنْ عَائِشَةَ، قَالَتْ كُنْتُ أَشْرَبُ وَأَنَا حَائِضٌ، ثُمَّ أُنَاوِلُهُ النَّبِيَّ صلى الله عليه وسلم فَيَضَعُ فَاهُ عَلَى مَوْضِعِ فِيَّ فَيَشْرَبُ وَأَتَعَرَّقُ الْعَرْقَ وَأَنَا حَائِضٌ ثُمَّ أُنَاوِلُهُ النَّبِيَّ صلى الله عليه وسلم فَيَضَعُ فَاهُ عَلَى مَوْضِعِ فِيَّ . وَلَمْ يَذْكُرْ زُهَيْرٌ فَيَشْرَبُ

Aisha reported: I would drink when I was menstruating, then I would hand it (the vessel) to the Apostle (ﷺ) and he would put his mouth where mine had been, and drink, and I would eat flesh from a bone when I was menstruating, then hand it over to the Apostle (ﷺ) and he would put his mouth where mine had been. Zuhair made no mention of (the Holy Prophet's) drinking.

The Blissful Union ©2017 Syed ISBN 978-93-5268-923-1

Reciting Quran reclining of your spouse's lap

Imam Muslim narrated in his *Saheeh* no. 301:

عَنْ عَائِشَةَ، أَنَّهَا قَالَتْ كَانَ رَسُولُ اللَّهِ صلى الله عليه وسلم يَتَّكِئُ فِي حِجْرِي وَأَنَا حَائِضٌ فَيَقْرَأُ الْقُرْآنَ

Aisha reported: The Messenger of Allah (ﷺ) would recline in my lap when I was menstruating, and recite the Qur'an.

The Blissful Union ©2017 Syed ISBN 978-93-5268-923-1

Combing your husband's hair

Imam Muslim narrated in his *Saheeh* no. 297:

عَنْ عَائِشَةَ، قَالَتْ كَانَ النَّبِيُّ صلى الله عليه وسلم إِذَا اعْتَكَفَ يُدْنِي إِلَىَّ رَأْسَهُ فَأُرَجِّلُهُ وَكَانَ لاَ يَدْخُلُ الْبَيْتَ إِلاَّ لِحَاجَةِ الإِنْسَانِ

It is reported from 'Aisha that she observed: When the Messenger of Allah (ﷺ) was in *I'tikaf*, he inclined his head towards me and I combed his hair, and he did not enter the house but for the natural calls (for relieving himself).

The Blissful Union ©2017 Syed ISBN 978-93-5268-923-1

Sensing the feelings of your spouse

Imam Al-Bukhari narrated in his *Saheeh* no. 5228:

عَنْ عَائِشَةَ ـ رضى الله عنها ـ قَالَتْ قَالَ لِي رَسُولُ اللَّهِ صلى الله عليه وسلم " إِنِّي لأَعْلَمُ إِذَا كُنْتِ عَنِّي رَاضِيَةً، وَإِذَا كُنْتِ عَلَىَّ غَضْبَى ". قَالَتْ فَقُلْتُ مِنْ أَيْنَ تَعْرِفُ ذَلِكَ فَقَالَ " أَمَّا إِذَا كُنْتِ عَنِّي رَاضِيَةً فَإِنَّكِ تَقُولِينَ لاَ وَرَبِّ مُحَمَّدٍ، وَإِذَا كُنْتِ غَضْبَى قُلْتِ لاَ وَرَبِّ إِبْرَاهِيمَ ". قَالَتْ قُلْتُ أَجَلْ وَاللَّهِ يَا رَسُولَ اللَّهِ، مَا أَهْجُرُ إِلاَّ اسْمَكَ.

Narrated Aisha: That Allah's Messenger (ﷺ) said to her, "I know when you are pleased with me or angry with me." I said, "Whence do you know that?" He said, "When you are pleased with me, you say, 'No, by the Lord of Muhammad,' but when you are angry with me, then you say, 'No, by the Lord of Abraham.' " Thereupon I said, "Yes (you are right), but by Allah, O Allah's Messenger (ﷺ), I leave nothing but your name."

The Blissful Union ©2017 Syed ISBN 978-93-5268-923-1

Know emotional changes in women during menses

Messenger of Allah (ﷺ) said in *hadith* reported in *Saheeh Muslim* no.1208 :

فَاتَّقُوا اللَّهَ فِي النِّسَاءِ فَإِنَّكُمْ أَخَذْتُمُوهُنَّ بِأَمَانِ اللَّهِ

"Fear Allah concerning women! Verily you have taken them on the security of Allah."

Woman's body goes through various physical and emotional changes during different phases of menstruation cycle. Emotional symptoms may include: feelings of anxiety, irritability or depression. According to research by Dr. Ed Keogh and team in 2014 published in journal for the international association for study of pain called *"Pain"*, periods (menstruation) decrease cognitive ability in women .The abdominal pain, backaches, and nausea during a woman's period can actually affect how she thinks and feels, reducing her cognitive ability.

Knowing PMS and PMDD

"PMS," stands for premenstrual syndrome and "PMDD" stands for "premenstrual dysphoric disorder".

PMS is a specific, reoccurring and relatively severe set of symptoms that occur during the premenstrual phase of a woman's cycle. Some of the symptoms of PMS and PMDD experienced by almost every woman are: depression, angry outbursts, irritability, anxiety, confusion, withdrawal from people, bloating and headache. Every woman is different. One might have horrible mood swings while another just seems depressed. One might crave chocolate while another loses her appetite. Sometimes they burst into tears for no reason.

Some of the things men can do to make her feel better are:

1) Give her compliments. Say things that will make her feel happy.
2) Take the stress off her by helping her out in house hold work. Messenger of Allah (ﷺ) used to help his wives with house hold work.
3) Give comfort to her by a warm hug.
4) Make her feel loved and appreciated and let her know how happy you are to have her in your life.

Rights of Wife

Allah says in Al-Quran (2:228):

وَلَهُنَّ مِثْلُ ٱلَّذِى عَلَيْهِنَّ بِٱلْمَعْرُوفِ ۚ وَلِلرِّجَالِ عَلَيْهِنَّ دَرَجَةٌ ۗ وَٱللَّهُ عَزِيزٌ حَكِيمٌ

And they (women) have rights (over their husbands as regards living expenses) similar (to those of their husbands) over them (as regards obedience and respect) to what is reasonable, but men have a degree (of responsibility) over them. And Allah is All-Mighty, All-Wise.

Shaykh Abdurrahman As-Saadi said in *Tafseer* of this *ayah* in *Tayseer Al-Kareem* (1/167):

أي: وللنساء على بعولتهن من الحقوق واللوازم مثل الذي عليهن لأزواجهن من الحقوق اللازمة والمستحبة. ومرجع الحقوق بين الزوجين يرجع إلى المعروف، وهو: العادة الجارية في ذلك البلد وذلك الزمان من مثلها لمثله، ويختلف ذلك باختلاف الأزمنة والأمكنة، والأحوال، والأشخاص والعوائد.

وفي هذا دليل على أن النفقة والكسوة، والمعاشرة، والمسكن، وكذلك الوطء - الكل يرجع إلى المعروف، فهذا موجب العقد المطلق. وأما مع الشرط، فعلى شرطهما، إلا شرطا أحل حراما، أو حرم حلالا.

They have similar rights over them to what is reasonable, that is, wives have the same rights over their husbands as the husbands have over their wives. The real source of the rights of a husband and wife towards each other is *ma'ruf* (enjoying

The Blissful Union ©2017 Syed ISBN 978-93-5268-923-1

good), which here imply the customs and traditions regarding husbands and wives that are popular in that era and in the particular region or city. Popular customs keep changing according to the changing times, traditions and conditions.
The noble verse is a proof that the source for deriving decisions about all matters of living, dressing, social commitment, home life and the intimate and special relationship of a husband and wife is *ma'ruf*. This is only valid for *al-aqd al-mutlaq* (contract without any conditions) where no pre-conditions were set at the time of the marriage, as for the contract which is not absolute and contains some preconditions, then those terms and conditions will be followed. However, there must not be any pre-conditions in this contract which violate the religious commandments of what is permissible and impermissible.

Imam Abu Dawood reported in his *Sunan* no. 2142 under chapter:

باب فِي حَقِّ الْمَرْأَةِ عَلَى زَوْجِهَا

Chapter: The Rights Of A Woman Upon Her Husband

عَنْ حَكِيمِ بْنِ مُعَاوِيَةَ الْقُشَيْرِيِّ، عَنْ أَبِيهِ، قَالَ قُلْتُ يَا رَسُولَ اللَّهِ مَا حَقُّ زَوْجَةِ أَحَدِنَا عَلَيْهِ قَالَ " أَنْ تُطْعِمَهَا إِذَا طَعِمْتَ وَتَكْسُوَهَا إِذَا اكْتَسَيْتَ - أَوِ اكْتَسَبْتَ - وَلاَ تَضْرِبِ الْوَجْهَ وَلاَ تُقَبِّحْ وَلاَ تَهْجُرْ إِلاَّ فِي الْبَيْتِ " . قَالَ أَبُو دَاوُدَ " وَلاَ تُقَبِّحْ أَنْ تَقُولَ قَبَّحَكِ اللَّهُ " .

Narrated Mu'awiyah al-Qushayri : Mu'awiyah asked: Messenger of Allah, what is the right of the wife of one of us over him? He replied: That you should give her food when you eat, clothe her when you clothe yourself, do not strike her

on the face, do not revile her or separate yourself from her except in the house.
Abu Dawood said: The meaning of "do not revile her" is, as you say: "May Allah revile you".

Shaykh Ibn Uthaymeen explained this *hadith* in *Sharh Riyadh as-Saliheen* (3/131):

وهنا سأله معاوية ((ما حق امرأة أحدنا عليه؟ قال: ((أن تطعمها إذا طعمت، وتكسوها إذا اكتسيت)) يعني لا تخص نفسك بالكسوة دونها، ولا بالطعام دونها؛ بل هي شريكة لك يجب عليك أن تنفق عليها كما تنفق على نفسك، حتى إن كثيراً من العلماء يقول: إذا لم ينفق الرجل على زوجته وطالبت بالفسخ عند القاضي؛ فللقاضي أن يفسخ النكاح؛ لأنه قصر بحقها الواجب لها

And here Mu'awiyah asked him: (What is the right of the wife of one of us over him? He replied: That you should give her food when you eat, clothe her when you clothe yourself) meaning don't only think of yourself when it comes to clothing or food (leaving her out), verily she is your partner (she has a right over that which you do for yourself from spending) it is obligatory upon you to spend on her like you spend on yourself. Many of the scholars say: If a man does not spend on his wife and she asks for nullification of the *Nikah* from the judge, then it is upon the judge to nullify the *Nikah*, because the husband fell short in fulfilling what was obligatory upon him from her rights.

Spending on your wife and family is a source of reward from Allah

Its reported in *Saheeh Al-Bukhari* no. 56 that Messenger of Allah (ﷺ) said:

"إِنَّكَ لَنْ تُنْفِقَ نَفَقَةً تَبْتَغِي بِهَا وَجْهَ اللَّهِ إِلَّا أُجِرْتَ عَلَيْهَا حَتَّى مَا تَجْعَلُ فِي فَمِ امْرَأَتِكَ"

"You will be rewarded for whatever you spend for Allah's sake even if it were a morsel which you put in your wife's mouth."

Imam Muslim narrated in his Saheeh no. 995 that Messenger of Allah (ﷺ) said:

" دِينَارٌ أَنْفَقْتَهُ فِي سَبِيلِ اللَّهِ وَدِينَارٌ أَنْفَقْتَهُ فِي رَقَبَةٍ وَدِينَارٌ تَصَدَّقْتَ بِهِ عَلَى مِسْكِينٍ وَدِينَارٌ أَنْفَقْتَهُ عَلَى أَهْلِكَ أَعْظَمُهَا أَجْرًا الَّذِي أَنْفَقْتَهُ عَلَى أَهْلِكَ "

Of the dinar you spend as a contribution in Allah's path, or to set free a slave, or as a *Sadaqa* given to a needy, or to support your family, the one yielding the greatest reward is that which you spent on your family.

Wife's right to intimacy and being away from wife for a long period of time

There is an authentic *hadith* reported by Imam Al-Bukhari in his *Saheeh* no.5199 under chapter : بَاب لِزَوْجِكَ عَلَيْكَ حَقٌّ

Chapter: Your wife has a right over you. Messenger of Allah (ﷺ) said

" فَإِنَّ لِجَسَدِكَ عَلَيْكَ حَقًّا ، وَإِنَّ لِعَيْنِكَ عَلَيْكَ حَقًّا ، وَإِنَّ لِزَوْجِكَ عَلَيْكَ حَقًّا ".

Your body has a right over you, your eyes have a right over you and your wife has a right over you."

Imam Al-Bayhaqi in *As-Sunan Al-Kubra* (9/51) no.17850 with an authentic chain that:

خَرَجَ عُمَرُ بْنُ الْخَطَّابِ رَضِيَ اللهُ عَنْهُ مِنَ اللَّيْلِ، فَسَمِعَ امْرَأَةً تَقُولُ :
تَطَاوَلَ هَذَا اللَّيْلُ وَاسْوَدَّ جَانِبُهْ ... وَأَرَّقَنِي أَنْ لَا حَبِيبَ أُلَاعِبُهْ
فَقَالَ عُمَرُ بْنُ الْخَطَّابِ رَضِيَ اللهُ عَنْهُ لِحَفْصَةَ بِنْتِ عُمَرَ رَضِيَ اللهُ عَنْهَا: " كَمْ أَكْثَرُ مَا تَصْبِرُ الْمَرْأَةُ عَنْ زَوْجِهَا؟ ". فَقَالَتْ: سِتَّةٌ أَوْ أَرْبَعَةُ أَشْهُرٍ. فَقَالَ عُمَرُ رَضِيَ اللهُ عَنْهُ: " لَا أَحْبِسُ الْجَيْشَ أَكْثَرَ مِنْ هَذَا"

Once Umar bin Al-Khattab (may Allah be pleased with him) was walking during the night, he heard a woman saying: "What a long night filled with darkness! I do not have a lover with whom I can play. So he asked his daughter Hafsa (may Allah be pleased with her) .How long can a woman stay away from her husband? She said: six or four months. So Umar (may Allah be pleased with him) said: I will not withhold the army more than this!

The lady spoken about in this incident and her need for her husband shows how serious and important this matter is. A woman will be able to live with her husband even if he is not able to provide her one or some of her necessities but she will definitely not be able to live with a husband who does not fulfill her right of intimacy and satisfying her sexually. It is even more difficult upon her if her husband is someone who stays away from her for long periods of time for this can create great *fitnah* for her by pushing her towards what is *haram*. For example; if he cannot spend on her to fulfill her needs she can do so by spending her own wealth but to satisfy her intimate needs no one can do this for her except her husband.
It is upon the husband to have intercourse with her according to his and her need and ability.

Shaykhul Islam Ibn Taymiyyah said in *Majmoo' al-Fataawa* (32/271):

يجب على الرجل أن يطأ زوجته بالمعروف ، وهو من أوكد حقها عليه ، أعظم من إطعامها

It is obligatory upon the man to have intercourse with his wife on a reasonable basis, and it is one of the most important rights that she has over him; it is a right greater than feeding her.

The Blissful Union ©2017 Syed ISBN 978-93-5268-923-1

Rights of husband

He is your paradise or hell-fire...

Imam Ahmad bin Hanbal narrated in his *Musnad* no.19003 with sound chain of narration:

عَنِ الْحُصَيْنِ بْنِ مِحْصَنٍ، أَنَّ عَمَّةً لَهُ أَتَتِ النَّبِيَّ صَلَّى اللهُ عَلَيْهِ وَسَلَّمَ فِي حَاجَةٍ، فَفَرَغَتْ مِنْ حَاجَتِهَا، فَقَالَ لَهَا النَّبِيُّ صَلَّى اللهُ عَلَيْهِ وَسَلَّمَ: «أَذَاتُ زَوْجٍ أَنْتِ؟» قَالَتْ: نَعَمْ، قَالَ: «كَيْفَ أَنْتِ لَهُ؟» قَالَتْ: مَا آلُوهُ إِلَّا مَا عَجَزْتُ عَنْهُ، قَالَ: «فَانْظُرِي أَيْنَ أَنْتِ مِنْهُ، فَإِنَّمَا هُوَ جَنَّتُكِ وَنَارُكِ»

Hussain bin Mihsan's paternal aunt came to the Prophet and he dealt with her need then Prophet (ﷺ) asked: "Do you have a husband?" She said, "Yes." He said: "How are you with him?" She said, "I do not neglect any of his rights except those I am unable to fulfill."Prophet (ﷺ) said, Evaluate yourself concerning your husband for he is your paradise or hell-fire. Meaning he is the cause of you entering paradise if you fulfill his rights and the cause of your entering hell if you fall short in that.

Obedience to husband

Imam Ibn Hibban narrated a sound *hadith* in his *Saheeh* no.4163 that Messenger of Allah (ﷺ) said:

إِذَا صَلَّتِ الْمَرْأَةُ خُمُسَهَا، وَصَامَتْ شَهْرَهَا، وَحَصَّنَتْ فَرْجَهَا، وَأَطَاعَتْ بَعْلَهَا،"
"دخلت من أي أبواب الجنة شاءت

"If a woman prays her five (daily prayers), fasts her month (Ramadan), guards her private parts and obeys her husband, it will be said to her: 'Enter Paradise from whichever of the gates of Paradise you wish'.

Being grateful to him

Imam Nasa'ee narrated an authentic *hadith* in his *As-Sunan Al-Kubra* 9086 that Messenger of Allah (ﷺ) said:

لَا يَنْظُرُ اللهُ إِلَى امْرَأَةٍ لَا تَشْكُرُ لِزَوْجِهَا وَهِيَ لَا تَسْتَغْنِي عَنْهُ

"Allah will not look at a woman who is ungrateful to her husband, while she is unable to do without him."

Seeking his permission

Its reported in *Saheeh Al-Bukhari* 5195 :

عَنْ أَبِي هُرَيْرَةَ، رضى الله عنه أَنَّ رَسُولَ اللَّهِ صلى الله عليه وسلم قَالَ " لاَ يَحِلُّ لِلْمَرْأَةِ أَنْ تَصُومَ وَزَوْجُهَا شَاهِدٌ إِلاَّ بِإِذْنِهِ، وَلاَ تَأْذَنَ فِي بَيْتِهِ إِلاَّ بِإِذْنِهِ، وَمَا أَنْفَقَتْ مِنْ نَفَقَةٍ عَنْ غَيْرِ أَمْرِهِ فَإِنَّهُ يُؤَدَّى إِلَيْهِ شَطْرُهُ ". وَرَوَاهُ أَبُو الزِّنَادِ أَيْضًا عَنْ مُوسَى عَنْ أَبِيهِ عَنْ أَبِي هُرَيْرَةَ فِي الصَّوْمِ

"Narrated Abu Huraira: Allah's Messenger (ﷺ) said, It is not lawful for a lady to fast (*Nawafil*) without the permission of her husband when he is at home; and she should not allow anyone to enter his house except with his permission; and if she spends of his wealth (on charitable purposes) without being ordered by him, he will get half of the reward."

Spending his wealth wisely

It is reported in *Jami at-Tirmidhi* no 670 with sound chain:

عَنْ أَبِي أُمَامَةَ الْبَاهِلِيِّ، قَالَ سَمِعْتُ رَسُولَ اللَّهِ صلى الله عليه وسلم فِي خُطْبَتِهِ عَامَ حَجَّةِ الْوَدَاعِ يَقُولُ " لاَ تُنْفِقُ امْرَأَةٌ شَيْئًا مِنْ بَيْتِ زَوْجِهَا إِلاَّ بِإِذْنِ زَوْجِهَا " . قِيلَ يَا رَسُولَ اللَّهِ وَلاَ الطَّعَامُ قَالَ " ذَاكَ أَفْضَلُ أَمْوَالِنَا "

"Abu Umamah Al-Bahili said: "During a sermon of his in the year of the Farewell Hajj, I heard the Messenger of Allah say: 'A woman is not to spend anything from her husbands house without her husband's permission.' They said: O Messenger of Allah! What about food?' He said: 'That is our most virtuous wealth."

It is reported in *Saheeh Al-Bukhari* no.5364:

عَنْ عَائِشَةَ، أَنَّ هِنْدَ بِنْتَ عُتْبَةَ، قَالَتْ يَا رَسُولَ اللَّهِ إِنَّ أَبَا سُفْيَانَ رَجُلٌ شَحِيحٌ، وَلَيْسَ يُعْطِينِي مَا يَكْفِينِي وَوَلَدِي، إِلاَّ مَا أَخَذْتُ مِنْهُ وَهْوَ لاَ يَعْلَمُ فَقَالَ " خُذِي مَا يَكْفِيكِ وَوَلَدَكِ بِالْمَعْرُوفِ "

"Narrated Aisha: Hind bint `Utba said, "O Allah's Messenger (ﷺ)! Abu Sufyan is a miser and he does not give me what is sufficient for me and my children. Can I take of his property without his knowledge?" The Prophet (ﷺ) said, "Take what is sufficient for you and your children, and the amount should be just and reasonable."

Asking for divorce without a valid reason

There is a an authentic *hadith* reported in *Sunan Abu Dawood* no. 2226 that Messenger of Allah (ﷺ) said:

أَيُّمَا امْرَأَةٍ سَأَلَتْ زَوْجَهَا طَلاَقًا فِي غَيْرِ مَا بَأْسٍ فَحَرَامٌ عَلَيْهَا رَائِحَةُ الْجَنَّةِ

"If any woman asks her husband for divorce without some strong reason, the odour of Paradise will be forbidden to her."

Hafidh Ibn Hajr explained this *hadith* in *Fath al-Bari* (9/402):

الأخبار الواردة في ترهيب المرأة من طلب طلاق زوجها ، محمولة على إذا لم يكن بسبب يقتضي ذلك

"The narrations reported which warn women against asking for divorce from their husbands are to be understood as applying to cases where there is no reason for that."

Nowadays, this has become very common amongst muslim men and women around the world. Couples seek divorce for the slightest of tiff in their marital lives which could have been easily solved between themselves. It is shocking to see that especially women ask for divorce for reasons such as their husbands spending too much time on their phones or laptops or they did not like the way their husband dresses.

Refusing intimacy with husband

The Blissful Union ©2017 Syed ISBN 978-93-5268-923-1

Its reported in *Saheeh Al-Bukhari* no. 3237 that Messenger of Allah (ﷺ) said:

" إِذَا دَعَا الرَّجُلُ امْرَأَتَهُ إِلَى فِرَاشِهِ فَأَبَتْ، فَبَاتَ غَضْبَانَ عَلَيْهَا، لَعَنَتْهَا الْمَلاَئِكَةُ حَتَّى تُصْبِحَ "

"If a husband calls his wife to his bed (i.e. to have sexual relation) and she refuses and causes him to sleep in anger, the angels will curse her till morning."

This is because Islam condemn illicit sexual relations, fornication, adultery, prostitution, pornography and promiscuity. It is for this reason that a wife is bound to fulfill her husband's sexual desires so as to prevent him from straying.

Righteous Wife is the best joy of this world

Allah says in Al-Quran (4:33):

فَٱلصَّـٰلِحَـٰتُ قَـٰنِتَـٰتٌ حَـٰفِظَـٰتٌ لِّلْغَيْبِ بِمَا حَفِظَ ٱللَّهُ

"Therefore righteous women are devoutly obedient (to Allah and to their husbands), and guard in the husband's absence what Allah orders them to guard (e.g. their chastity, their husband's property)."

Imam Muslim narrated in his *Saheeh* no. 715 under the chapter.

باب خَيْرُ مَتَاعِ الدُّنْيَا الْمَرْأَةُ الصَّالِحَةُ

"Chapter: The best temporary joy of this world is a righteous woman."

عَنْ عَبْدِ اللَّهِ بْنِ عَمْرٍو، أَنَّ رَسُولَ اللَّهِ صلى الله عليه وسلم قَالَ " الدُّنْيَا مَتَاعٌ وَخَيْرُ مَتَاعِ الدُّنْيَا الْمَرْأَةُ الصَّالِحَةُ

"Abdullah bin Amr reported Allah's Messenger (ﷺ) as saying: The whole world is a provision, and the best of benefit of the world is the pious woman."

Shaykh Ibn Uthaymeen explained this *hadith* in *Sharh Riyadh as-Saliheen* (3/136-137): "If a person finds righteous wife with sound intellect and righteousness then this is the best kind of the provision in this world because she will keep his secret and protect his wealth and children. If a woman is sound in her intellect then she will manage his house properly and raise her kids in the best manner. If he looks at her, she pleases him and she protects herself in his absence. If he entrusts her with something then she is not treacherous. So this is the woman who is best provision in this world."

The Blissful Union ©2017 Syed ISBN 978-93-5268-923-1

Wife mixing with husband's relatives

From righteousness of the wife is that she keeps herself modest and chaste as *Haya* (bashfulness) is a part of faith.

Imam Al-Bukhari narrated in his *Saheeh* no. 6118:

مَرَّ النَّبِيُّ صلى الله عليه وسلم عَلَى رَجُلٍ وَهْوَ يُعَاتِبُ فِي الْحَيَاءِ يَقُولُ إِنَّكَ لَتَسْتَحْيِي. حَتَّى كَأَنَّهُ يَقُولُ قَدْ أَضَرَّ بِكَ. فَقَالَ رَسُولُ اللَّهِ صلى الله عليه وسلم " دَعْهُ فَإِنَّ الْحَيَاءَ مِنَ الإِيمَانِ

The Prophet (ﷺ) passed by a man who was admonishing his brother regarding *Haya'* (pious shyness from committing religious indiscretions) and was saying, "You are very shy, and I am afraid that might harm you." On that, Allah's Messenger (ﷺ) said, "Leave him, for *Haya'* is (a part) of Faith."

From *Haya* is that she refrains from freely mixing with the male relatives of her husband and in general those males who are impermissible for her. It is not allowed for a woman to be alone with his male relatives.

Imam Al-Bukhari narrated in his *Saheeh* no. 3006:

عَنِ ابْنِ عَبَّاسٍ ـ رضى الله عنهما ـ أَنَّهُ سَمِعَ النَّبِيَّ صلى الله عليه وسلم يَقُولُ " لاَ يَخْلُوَنَّ رَجُلٌ بِامْرَأَةٍ، وَلاَ تُسَافِرَنَّ امْرَأَةٌ إِلاَّ وَمَعَهَا مَحْرَمٌ

Narrated Ibn `Abbas: That he heard the Prophet (ﷺ) saying, "It is not permissible for a man to be alone with a woman, and no lady should travel except with a *Mahram* (i.e. her husband or a person whom she cannot marry in any case for ever; e.g. her father, brother, etc.)."

Being alone with someone who is impermissible for her can make the path to sin and immorality easy.

Imam Al-Bukhari narrates in his *Saheeh* no. 5232:

عَنْ عُقْبَةَ بْنِ عَامِرٍ، أَنَّ رَسُولَ اللَّهِ صلى الله عليه وسلم قَالَ " إِيَّاكُمْ وَالدُّخُولَ عَلَى النِّسَاءِ ". فَقَالَ رَجُلٌ مِنَ الأَنْصَارِ يَا رَسُولَ اللَّهِ أَفَرَأَيْتَ الْحَمْوَ. قَالَ " الْحَمْوُ الْمَوْتُ ".

Narrated Uqba bin 'Amir: Allah's Messenger (ﷺ) said, "Beware of entering upon the ladies." A man from the Ansar said, "Allah's Apostle! What about *Al-Hamu* the in-laws of the wife (the brothers of her husband or his nephews etc.)?" The Prophet (ﷺ) replied: The in-laws of the wife are death itself.

Shaykh Ibn Uthaymeen explained above *hadith* in *Sharh Riyadh as-Saliheen* (6/368).Here is a summarization of what he said:

Al-Hamw are the brothers, uncles from father's and mother's side (of a husband) , these are from the *Hamw* and they are not from her *Maharim* (those who are permissible for her to interact with). As for the father of the husband and his sons they are permissible for her to mix with.

The Messenger (ﷺ) has emphasized strongly about mixing with the husband's male relatives and he has warned them from entering upon the wife in the absence of a *Mahram*. As a

The Blissful Union ©2017 Syed ISBN 978-93-5268-923-1

person runs away from death, similarly, the wife should stay away as much as she can from the male relatives of her husband and this is evidence for a strong admonition. The husband's relatives entering upon the wife in the absence of a *Mahram* is more dangerous for them than any other stranger because they are considered as relatives, so people do not deem this to be something wrong. They have taken this matter so lightly to the point that the husband leaves his wife alone with his brother while he leaves the house for work and this is *Haram* because Satan runs through the veins of children of Adam. End of quote.

Every kind of sin leads a person to gain the wrath of Allah and the more severe the admonition, the more painful the torment. It is upon the relatives of the husband to ask permission before entering his house and they should go back without feeling any kind of negative feelings upon being asked to leave. And it is upon the wife that she does not let any *non-Mahram* enter her house in the absence of her *Mahram*.

So take heed, O Sisters in Islam. Protection of your chastity is protection of your *Deen* which in turns leads to strengthening the bond of marriage and love between you and your spouse. For the one who takes a step in the way of Allah to please Him not worrying about displeasing others, Allah will be in their aid and Allah will bless them in ways they have never imagined.

The Blissful Union ©2017 Syed ISBN 978-93-5268-923-1

Conclusion:

We sincerely hope that reader has benefited from this book and pray that he/she is able to implement what is explained in order to find happiness in this life and the next.

We felt that it was of paramount importance that Muslims acquire authentic Islamic knowledge and that they do not shy away from learning matters related to intimacy due to cultural taboos.

If we said anything correct, then it is from Allah, and if we erred, then that is from ourselves and Satan.

The Blissful Union ©2017 Syed ISBN 978-93-5268-923-1

Glossary of Islamic terms

Deen: Religion of Islam.
Dua: invocation; supplication
Fiqh: the understanding and application of the *Sharee'ah* from its sources
Fatwa (pl. Fataawa): religious verdict
Fitnah: includes meanings of testing and trial.
Hadith: "a saying, action or tacit approval ascribed to the Prophet"
Haram: Impermissible or prohibited in Islam. It is that for which the one who does it will be punished and the one who abstains from it will be rewarded, if the reason for his abstinence is following the prohibition of Allah.

Ibaadah: worship; worship of Allah

Imam: leader; scholar of Islam; leader of a state

In-sha-Allah: "God willing" or "if Allah wills".

Mahram: It refers to all those males whom a woman cannot marry at anytime in her life whatsoever. (i.e. one's father, brother, father in-law, son etc).

Mufassir: Exegete or an interpreter of Al-Quran.

Sahabi: (companion) He is someone who saw the Prophet (ﷺ) and believed in him as well as died a Muslim.

Salaf: predecessors; the early Muslims; the Muslims of the first three generations: the *Companions*, the *Successors* and their successors

Sharee'ah: Islamic legislation.

Sunnah: Linguistically it means a practice. In legislative definition, Sunnah is defined as "Statements, actions or tacit approvals of Prophet".

Tabi'een: generation of Muslims who were born after the passing of the Prophet Muhammad but who were contemporaries of the Sahaba (companions).

Tafseer: Commentary or an explanation of Al-Quran.

Taqwa: Fear of Allah (God consciousness). It includes doing everything that Allah has enjoined whether it is obligatory, recommended, and avoiding all that He has forbidden, whether it is haram (forbidden) or disliked.

Umm: mother of; used as a means of identification

Ummah: community or nation, used to refer global community of Muslims.

Bibliography

1. The Noble Quran: Interpretation of the Meanings of the Noble Qur'an in the English Language (English and Arabic Edition). Translated by Muhammad Muhsin Khan, Muhammad Taqi-ud-Din Al-Hilali

2. Jaami Al-Bayaan (Tafseer At-Tabari) by Abu Jafar Muhammd bin Jareer At- Tabari edited by Ahmad Muhammad Shakir published by Ar-Risaalah in 1420H and revised later.

3. Fath Al-Qadeer by Muhammad bin Ali Ash-Shawkani Al-Yemeni published by Dar Ibn Kathir Damascus in 1414 H and revised later.

4. Al-Jaami li-Ahkaam Al-Quran by Abu Abdillah Muhammad bin Ahmad Al-Qurtubi edited by Ahmad Al-Burduni published by Dar Al-Kutub Al-Misriyyah Cairo in 1384 H and revised later.

5. Tafsir Ibn Katheer by Abul Fida Ismaeel bin Umar Bin Kathir edited by Saami bin Muhammad published by Dar Tayba in 1420 H and revised later.

6. Tafseer As-Saadi by Abdurrahman bin Naasir As-Saadi translated by S. Abd al-Hamid published by Islamic literary foundation.

7. Tafsir Ibn Katheer by Abul Fida Ismaeel bin Umar Bin Kathir (English) translated and published by Darussalam in 10 volumes.

8. Sahih Al-Bukhari by Imam Muhammad bin Ismaeel Al-Bukhari (Arabic / English) (9 Volumes) Translated by : Dr. Muhammad Mushin Khan. Darussalam

9. Sahih Muslim By Imam Muslim bin Hujjaj (Arabic / English) (7 Volumes). Darussalam.

10. Jami At Tirmidhi by Imam Abu Eesa Muhammad bin Eesaa(Arabic/English) (6 Volumes) Translated by: Abu Khaliyl. Darussalam.

11. Sunan Abu Dawud by Imam Abu Dawud Sulaiman Bin Ashath (Arabic/English) (5 Volumes) Translated by: Abu Ammar Yasir Qadhi. Darussalam.

12. Sunan Ibn Majah by Imam Muhammad ibn Majah Al-Qazwini (Arabic/English) (5 Volumes) Translated by: Nasiruddin al-Khattab. Darussalam.

13. Sunan Al-Kubra by Imam Abu Abdur-Rahman Ahmad bin Shu'ayb bin Bahr An-Nasai edited by Hasan Abdul-Munim Shilby published by Ar-Risaalah, Beirut in 1421H and revised later.

14. Sunan An-Nasai by Imam Abu Abdur-Rahman Ahmad bin Shu'ayb bin Bahr An-Nasai (Arabic/English) (6 Volumes) Translated by: Nasiruddin al-Khattab. Darussalam.

15. Musnad Ahmad by Ahmad bin Muhammad bin Hanbal edited by Ahmad Shakir published by Dar Al-Hadith Cairo in 1416 H and revised later.

16. Al-Mu'jam Al-Kabeer by Abul Qasim Sulayman bin Ahmad at-Tabraanee edited by Hamdee Abdul Majeed Salafee published by Maktabah Ibn Taymiyyah Cairo in 1415 H and revised later.

17. Al-Mu'jam AlAwsat by Abul Qasim Sulayman bin Ahmad at-Tabraaneeedited by Tariq bin Awadullah and Abdul Muhsin bin Ibrahim published by Dar Al-Harmayn Cairo in

18. As-Sunan Al-Kubra by Abu Bakr Ahmad bin Hussain Al-Bayhaqi edited by Muhammad Abdul Qadir published by Dar Al-Kutub Al-Ilmiyya Beirut in 1424 H and revised later.

19. Saheeh Ibn Hibban by Abu Hatim Muhammad bin Hibban Al-Busti edited by Shuayb al-Arnaoot published by Ar-Risaalah Beirut in 1414 H and revised later.

20. Al-Mustadrak Ala as-Saheehayn by Abu Abdillah Muhammad bin Abdillah Al-Haakim edited by Mustafa Abdul Qadir published by Dar Al-Kutub Al-Ilmiyyah Beirut published in 1411H and revised later

21. Al-Minhaj Sharh Saheeh Muslim bin Hujjaj by Abu Zakariya Yahya bin Sharf Al-Nawawi published by Dar Ihyaa At-Turaath Beirut in 1392 H and revised later.

22. Tuhfatul Ahwadee bi-Sharh Jaami At-Tirmidhi by Muhammad Abdurrahman bin Abdurrahim Al-Mubarakfoori published by Dar al-Kutub Al-Ilmiyyah Beirut in 1353 H and revised later.

23. Sharh Riyaad as-Saliheen by Muhammad bin Saleh bin Muhammad Al-Uthaymeen published by Dar Al-Watan Riyadh in 1426 and revised later.

24. Jaami Al-Uloom wal-Hikam by Abdurrahman bin Shihabuddin Abul Farj bin Rajab edited by Shuayb al-Arnaoot published by Ar-Risaalah in1419 H.

25. Majmoo' al-Fataawa by Taqeeuddin Abul Abbas Ahmad bin Abdul Haleem Ibn Taymiyyah edited by Abdurrahman bin Muhammad bin Qasim published by King Fahd Printing press Madeenah in 1416 H and revised many times.

26. Al-Haawi min Fataawaa al-Albaani (extracts translated by Ahmed Abu Turaab)

27. Tahdheeb Al-Kamaal fee Asmaa ar-Rijaal by Yusuf bin Abdurrahman Abul Hujjaj Al-Mizzee edited by Dr.Bashar Awaad published by Ar-Risaalah in 1400H and revised later.

28. Sayd al-Khatir by Abul Farj Abdurrahman bin Ali Al-Jawzi published by Dar Al-Qalam Damascus in 1425 H and revised later.

29. Hilyatul Awliya wa tabaqat al-Asfiya by Abu Nuaym Ahmad bin Abdullah al-Asbahaani published by Dar Al-Kutub Al-Ilmiyyah Beirut in 1409H.

30. Ash-Sharee'ah by Abu Bakr Muhammad bin Hussain Al-Ajury Al-Baghdadi edited by Dr. Abdullah bin Umar bin Sulayman published by Dar Al-Watan Riyadh in 1420 H and revised later.

31. Fatawah Islamiyah :Islamic Verdicts : (8 Volumes) by Shaykh Abdul Aziz bin Abdullah bin Baz, Shaykh Muhammad bin Salih Al Uthaimin, Shaykh Abdullah bin Abdur Rahman Al Jibreen translated by:

Muhammad bin Abdul Aziz al Musnad. Published by Darussalam

32. Al-Mughni by Abu Muhammad Muwaffaq al-Deen Abdullah bin Ahmad bin Muhammad bin Qudamah published Maktabah Al-Qahira in 1388 H.

33. Al-Awsat fee as-Sunan wal-Ijmaa wal-Ikhtilaaf by Imam Abu Bakr Muhammad bin Ibrahim bin Al-Mundhir edited by a group published by Dar Al-Falah in 1430H.

34. Al-Wafi bil-Wafayat by Salahuddin Khalil bin Aybak As-Safdi edited by Ahmad Arnaoot and Turki Mustafa published by Dar Ihyaa Ath-Turaath Beirut in 1420H.

35. Siyar A'laam An-Nubalaa by Shamshuddin Abu Abdillah Muhammad bin Ahmad Adh-Dhahabi edited by researchers under guidance of Shuayb al-Arnaoot published by Ar-Risaalah in 1405 H and revised later.

36. Tareekh Al-Madeenah by Umar bin Shuba bin Ubaydah Abu Zayd edited by Faheem Muhammad published in 1399 H.

37. Tareekh Dimashq by Abul Qasim Ali bin Hasan known as Ibn Asaakir published by Dar Al-Fikhr in 1415 H.

38. Age at marriage and marital instability: Revisiting the Becker-Landes-Michael hypothesis by Evelyn L Lehrer in Journal of Population Economics 21(2):463-484 · February 2008.

39. Later first marriage and marital success by Norval D. Glenn, Jeremy E. Uecker, Robert W.B. Love Jr published Social Science Research Volume 39, Issue 5, September 2010, Pages 787–800.

The Blissful Union ©2017 Syed ISBN 978-93-5268-923-1

40. For Richer, for poorer by W. Bradford Wilcox and Robert I. Lerman. Institute of Family studies.

41. The neural basis of romantic love by Bartels and Zeki S published in 11(17):3829-34 · December 2000.

42. Sexuality Now: Embracing Diversity, 5th Edition Janell L. Carroll University of Hartford Published in 2016.

43. "Human anatomy" by Kenneth Saladin published in 2010.

44. Sexual dysfunction in men with chronic prostatis/ chronic pelvic pain syndrome.Improvement after trigger point release and paradoxical relaxation training by Anderson RU, Wise D, Sawyer T and Chan CA published in Journal of Urology 2006 Oct;176(4 Pt 1):1534-8.

45. Pornography's Impact on Sexual Satisfaction by Dolf Zillmann and Jennings Bryant published in Journal of Applied social psychology volume 18, Issue 5 April 1988 Pages 438–453.

www.ingramcontent.com/pod-product-compliance
Lightning Source LLC
Chambersburg PA
CBHW062136160726
48282CB00027B/838